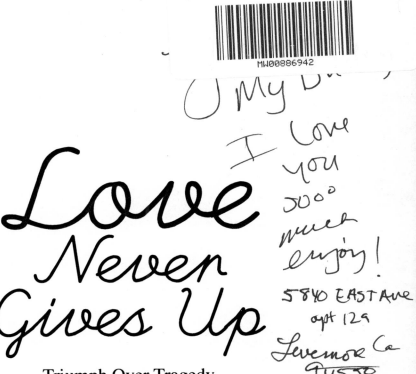

Love Never Gives Up

Triumph Over Tragedy, Through God's Unfailing Love

O My D...
I love
you
ooo
much
enjoy!

5840 EAST Ave
apt 129
Livermore Ca
~~94550~~
94550

Lisa C. Moreno

XULON PRESS

My hope and prayer for all those who read this book is that you will be able to overcome life's most difficult situations. Also that you will understand the love our Lord has for you—the love that never gives up.

1 Corinthians 13:7 (NLT)

"Love never gives up, never loses faith, is always hopeful, and endures through every circumstance."

Chapter 1

Exodus 20:5 (AMP)

*"You shall not bow down yourself to them or serve
them; for I the Lord your God am a jealous God, visiting the iniquity of the fathers upon the children to the
third and fourth generation of those who hate Me."*

Ephesians 6:12 (AMP)

*"For we are not wrestling with flesh and blood [con-
tending only with physical opponents], but against the
despotisms, against the powers, against [the master
spirits who are] the world rulers of this present darkness, against the spirit forces of wickedness in the
heavenly (supernatural) sphere."*

*W*hen I looked at my family's history, I saw patterns of behaviors that seemed to pass on to the next generations. My family had destructive behaviors like violence, adultery, depression, addiction, and more. These things seemed to filter down to the children. I didn't realize until later, after becoming a Christian, that this pattern was called a generational curse.

My earliest childhood memory is lying in bed, at about age three, waking up to demons surrounding my bed and touching me. It felt like a dream, but it was actually more like a nightmare.

Throughout my childhood, I constantly dealt with fear. It seemed as if fear ran in my family. I grew up in Oregon with my dad, Manuel; my Mom, Jesse; my younger sister, Patricia; and my little brother, Patrick. Mom dealt with many fears and panic at times, which stemmed mostly from her difficult childhood. Her father originally came from Mexico, but her Mexican mother was American-born. My mother described her dad as a very handsome, tall man with wild green eyes. She told me that he had stabbed my grandmother to near death and the authorities deported him back to Mexico. Mom was still very small then, and her mother remarried and conceived her ninth child.

When my grandmother went into labor, there were complications. She and the baby died. At age eight, mother had no one to parent her. She lived partly with relatives and other times in foster care.

My mother tells of having a natural intuition in regard to coming danger. This intuition helped her survive without parental guidance.

Along with this feeling of impending danger came an ungodly fear of the unknown. She felt afraid of tomorrow's happenings, violence, and death. These fears, at times, crippled her from moving forward in life. Mom passed her apprehension on to me. My fear-driven mentality grew similar to hers and haunted me throughout my childhood and into adulthood.

I also had to deal with anger throughout my life. Disdainful attitudes filled a major part of my family's daily lives and constantly consumed us. I have bad memories of my dad violently breaking things. He never hurt me, but had sudden outbursts of anger and would throw things across the room or get furious over little things; for example, when Mom made a dessert he didn't like. I remember times when I witnessed him hitting her. I felt terribly afraid and shrunk under the wrath of my father. Dad didn't like being corrected by anyone. We had to respond, "Yes, Daddy dear," and never speak our mind on anything we disagreed on, even if he was wrong. Although we feared Dad, I really loved him; he was very protective of us kids. So, although strict, he did show us affection.

We never experienced, as so many people have, weird things with my father, such as sexual abuse, and he always provided for his family. Dad nurtured us children and really loved babies. Even though he lacked merit, he always provided for us. My mom was loyal and faithful to him. Unlike my father, she rarely hugged or kissed us out of the blue. If we kissed her she'd let us, but she showed her love by accepting responsibilities and keeping a clean house.

9

One thing that really bothered me regarding my mom is how she let my dad intimidate her; she always looked afraid of him. His moods were unpredictable, and Mom always seemed to sense when his anger would rise up. My mom would walk on eggshells and it grieved me to see her that way. I did not see a loving hand toward my mom through my dad, except for his providing for her.

We saw addiction as normal in my home. Mom smoked weed ever since I could remember, and she suffered from depression. As my dad would go in and out of prison and battle a heroin addiction, I could tell it took a real toll on her emotions. Rarely did my mom drink, but when she did, it was horrible. I heard words towards me like "I hate you, it's all your fault." At the time I believed everything she said. As I said before, Mom drank only occasionally, but when she did, she turned into a violent and aggressive person. It was not a good thing for her or our family. Much later, she stopped drinking when she realized what she put us through.

At the age of five, while spending the night at a relative's home, I was put in a bed next to a teenage girl relative. She awakened me and forced me to touch her breasts. It didn't make sense to me as to why she would make me touch her. I felt confused and paralyzed with fear. The experience shocked me, but I kept silent. For some reason, I felt embarrassed. From then on, that experience made me question my sexuality and gave me unwarranted sexual thoughts. The molestation allowed a lot of, I believe, spiritual darkness in my life.

When I was about six years old, my Dad worked as a welder for a Native American reservation. One day, Dad had a terrible accident while welding. He was working on a module about twenty feet high on the top of a tank. His wire welding machine shot a hot wire into his glove and burned him. When he tried to shake off the burning wire, it stuck to his hand and he lost his balance.

Dad fell, and his forehead hit one of the tips of the rail. He hit the ground with all his might and yelled for Lyle—who was my father's co-worker and best friend. When Lyle had got to him; Dad's heart had stopped beating and he'd wet himself. Lyle called the ambulance and then called my mom to tell her that my dad had died. But, when the ambulance arrived, the paramedics brought him back to life with paddles. His heart failed three more times, and they brought him back each time. Dad stayed in a coma for the next two weeks.

When he woke up, he thought it was the 1960's and that Kennedy was president. So, in his mind, he was in his local hospital and was about fifteen years old. He recognized his parents and sisters, but didn't recognize my mom. When the doctor told him she was his wife, Dad said, "Wow, she's pretty. Ain't she, Doc? I did well for myself."

Later, my Dad's cousin, Rico, came down to see my dad. When Dad told him that he had unbearable head pain, Rico told my dad that he'd make him feel better. He gave Dad heroin while he was in the hospital. My father was vulnerable, not in his right mind, and Rico took advantage of the situation by asking my Dad personal questions. Dad trusted him, but later Rico robbed my Dad of everything he owned. This was the beginning of my Dad's thirty year addiction to heroin. His anger worsened and Mom's fear of him increased.

When I was about age six, my grandmother (a nice Catholic woman) lived near an elderly woman named Mrs. Morrow. I didn't know at the time, but she was a Christian woman and a pastor's wife. For some reason I always loved visiting her house. I remember feeling peace sitting still there on her couch. I wished I could have stayed in her home forever. Even as a small child I desired peace—something I'd never felt in my own life. I also remember, around the same time, my grandmother would play a cassette tape of someone speaking—it was an evangelist. The speaker's words about Jesus taking the keys of death and the grave from Satan, and preaching to those oppressed never left me. It was the first time I'd ever heard about anything Jesus did. The sermon had a drawing effect on me. I didn't know why, but his voice brought me peace and a hunger to learn more. I didn't know it was God's word that was captivating me. Traveling back home from my grandmother's house, I'd look out my car window. Often, I'd gaze at a beautiful, clear sky, filled with stars as far as my eye could see. I felt so in awe, and in thinking of the God who was still unrevealed to me, I would sing "Twinkle, Twinkle Little Star,"—the only song I knew to sing. **Now that I look back at times like this, I realize that God truly foreknew me and knew who I was going to become**.

When I was about eight years old, out bike riding, a man pulled up in a dark car and tried to talk to me. He appeared very scary to me. He wore dark sunglasses and looked about thirty years old. I had a terrible feeling he was going to try and take me. Mom had warned me what to do about things like this. She told me what to do if anyone ever tried to take me while I was riding my bike. Her exact words: "Drop your bike, scream, and run. If you leave your bike, I won't get mad at you." Word for word, I obeyed her advice. What my mom said spared my life. When I screamed, the man took off fast, and I ran in the house of my babysitter, crying. **They never found the man, but as time passed, God made me a protector of children and I now give them sound advice just as my mom had given me.**

One day I came home from school to see my mom's arm in bandages. She'd put her arm through the front door glass window. This had something to do with my dad, but I didn't know much; I just knew my mom was hurting. My mother, siblings, and I left our house and went to a shelter for women and children, located on the poor side of town. It was a huge house with several very old and dark rooms. Many mothers and their children seemed as dysfunctional as we were. My family stayed there for about three weeks, and I had to go to a new school.

I met a few little girls at school who had heard my last name and asked if my dad's name was Manuel. When I told them yes, one little girl responded, "My mom said your dad made a baby with another lady." I didn't understand this—I was still very naive about such things. She told me her name and I went back to the shelter and told my mom what the girl had said. Mom seemed to panic. We walked to a pay phone and she called the woman who had spread the rumor. I don't remember what Mom said, but I'm sure she sure gave her a piece of her mind.

We went back to the shelter and hurriedly packed up our things. Thinking of it now, that woman who spread the rumor probably would have kept spreading it and my dad would have found out where we stayed. This time we went farther away so my dad couldn't find us. I'm not sure how, but Mom somehow moved us into a more modern townhome. Oh, how I loved it there, and I had so much peace. Mom still had a cast on her arm, so I would comb her hair and help out a little more. I remember during that time I started to mature into a young lady, and Mom gave me more responsibility. However, she never complained about housekeeping or making dinners — she just did what needed to be done.

We simply led our lives. I went to a new school and made a few new friends. Sometime later, my dad's oldest sister came to visit us at our new home and asked if she could take me to California for a few months. My mom agreed, and I lived in California for three months without my family, and I attended another new school. While I was gone, my mom began the process of divorcing my dad. During the court hearing, Dad talked her out of the divorce and they got back together with the understanding they'd leave Oregon and start over again in California. My mom, dad, brother, sister, and I moved to Northern California when I was almost ten years old. How happy I felt, seeing my family again.

We lived with my aunt for a few more months and then moved to different city in California with another relative, for a short while. I once again started a new school, and as I recall, my dad was in jail while we stayed there. We lived out on a covered patio, and it felt weird for me to sleep outside. When my dad got out of jail, we once again moved to another city and, once more, a new school—in the ghetto. On the first day of school, I saw a young man beat up a school bus driver—and we lived there for about two years. I hated it.

One day Mom and I saw the police coming to the door. Mom whispered to me, "You know those funny plants we have in our room?" I said I did and she told me to go and hide them. The police asked about Dad, and mom tried to shut the door on them, but could not. While the police questioned Mom, I pulled my parents' marijuana plants by their roots and shoved them in my room's closet.

The police found halogen lamps, plant food and dead marijuana plants in my parent's bathroom, and all of it was confiscated. They came into my room and a policeman asked, "Do you have any plants in here?" I said, "No, and you can check if you don't believe me." The police took my word for it, and then left.

Now, my dad was gone most of the time. Things to take care of his heroin addiction. I often saw nice things in our house such as valuable coins, jewelry, VCRs, and more. One day, at about eleven years old, I remember waking up to find my dad almost dead by the kitchen sink. He had a needle sticking out of his arm and was foaming at the mouth. He looked asleep, but I couldn't rouse him. I screamed and Mom came, and, soon, the ambulance. I felt so frightened, I lost my breath. My dad lived, but the thought of him almost dying there greatly pained me. I had a terrible fear of him dying. Turned out, he had attempted suicide. Later, he told me he felt sorry about not being the husband Mom needed. We again moved back to our previous city and I, once again, started a new school. My dad returned to prison and had some gang affiliation there.

Once while in junior high, I went on a long trip with my mom and siblings to the prison where my dad was incarcerated. We went in my mom's little car. She hadn't much money—only enough for the gas home and a little food. The snow made it impossible to drive on, and Mom couldn't pay for a motel room. So we ended up going to a homeless shelter. I was terrified and had my eyes opened most of the night. The next morning my mom took us all to eat a hearty breakfast at very busy diner. She made us dine and dash.

Dad eventually got out of prison, and again he went back and forth between the streets and jail. He chose to be homeless, and would try countless drug rehabs, but would not change because he wasn't ready to change. Once out of prison, Dad acted lovey-dovey with Mom. He would make us many promises about how he would change and do right by us—none of which he fulfilled. Then, like a mad cycle, Mom became depressed again and slept a lot. We felt disappointed. The broken promises really hurt. It seemed like my dad would never change, and didn't care about us enough to want to change. My brother, sister, and I were growing up, living our lives. As teenagers, we found interests apart from waiting for my dad to change.

Dad would talk to my brother about prison and gangs and for some reason glorified it. My mom tried, with all the tools she had, to raise us right. Christmas time was so special in our home. Mom decorated the tree beautifully, and I could sit there for hours looking at it. I have fond memories of Christmas, settling down and relaxing with my mom. I remember how much a Christmas tree from Oregon meant to me; I can still smell the freshness. A Charlie Brown Christmas was my favorite Christmas cartoon and, to this day, watching it still brings me joy. My family did have each other. I didn't realize then how much it really cost my mom to raise us practically on her own. She probably couldn't have afforded the expensive, beautiful trees we always had. Mom scavenged for firewood as far back as I can remember. She walked down the railroad track and went behind buildings to find scrap wood to burn to heat our house. Somehow she managed to get the money for nice presents for us. She never bought herself stylish clothes or shoes; everything went to her kids. When we got old enough, my siblings and I worked for our things. My grandpa, my dad's dad, lived in the same city, and came to see us often. He was tall, big, and strong, and ran every day. He faithfully went to all of our important events and checked up on us weekly. We really needed him because his son couldn't be a good parent to us at that time. My grandpa has always shown us affection and we loved that about him. I was grateful to have a man I could count on to be there for me.

In between the ages of eleven and twelve, I stayed in a relatives' home, sleeping on the living room couch. A teenage female relative was supposed to be keeping an eye on me. Instead, she was with her boyfriend in her room all night, with the door closed. Her teenage brother, who was about seventeen years old, also lived there. He had bullied me for years and exercised control over me. In the middle of the night, I woke up to him fondling me. I was paralyzed with fear, just as with my sexual abuse at age five. When he realized I had awakened, he told me to go into a room with him, and I obeyed. There, he sexually abused me and he made me touch him. It felt like it lasted forever. Like a corpse, I lay there, waiting for it to end. At the time, I don't think I understood the ramifications of the attack. I simply felt confused, and wanted to forget it ever happened.

In junior high I met my best friend, Darla. We loved each other so much and went through a lot together. She endured some hard things growing up, but we had each other. At the age of about twelve or thirteen, we started playing Ouija board. We asked it many things and some bizarre things occurred. A very eerie thing happened as I stayed the night at my friend Darla's house—tormenting spirits shook every bed I laid on, and fear was with me every day. I saw things roll off a fireplace, and I slept with someone all the time or next to my mom on the floor by her bed. Even if I slept at another house, the tormenting spirits would follow. My mom knew this was happening, but she didn't know how to help me.

The shaking and torment continued until I received Christ as my savior.

At about age thirteen, I remember one day the young man who had previously fondled me had agreed to watch me and a relative of ours. This relative of ours was about a year younger than me. As I sat in the living room alone, watching TV, I realized her absence. I snuck quietly around the corner to find the brother had cornered this female relative. I heard him tell her, "Don't worry, we will be alone. I'll get rid of her." I flipped around the corner, and feeling bold, said with a firm voice, "You are not going to touch her! I know what you're thinking of doing!" He looked scared, and ran out the back door. She cried as I comforted her by wrapping her in my arms. I told her to sleep and that I would protect her. Since he lived there, I feared he would come back and bother us.

I didn't sleep that night, and kept watch over her. I never told anyone what happened because I didn't want to hurt the people in my family who I really cared about. I also felt that certain family members might not have believed me, so I kept my mouth shut. This young man was around 18 at the time that this happened. The female relative was about age 11 or 12.

As I grew older, I tried my mom's patience and would try to outwit her. Once at about thirteen, a friend invited me to spend the night, and her mom told my mom that she wouldn't let us leave the house. Mom didn't believe her, and sure enough, after calling to tell me goodnight, my friend's mom confessed that she let us go out to a party. My mom combed through every street looking for me and just when I was ready to step into the house where the party was held, my mom yelled out, "Lisa, get your ass in this car!"

My friends said, "See ya, Lisa!" I was busted!

My mom was smart, streetwise, and tough.

In school—Lord have mercy, I'm a little ashamed to say—I manipulated many of my teachers to get my way. I would tell them I had my period every other week and they couldn't possibly expect me to do any physical fitness activities. So that was my game. My goodness, I was a smooth talker.

I also had a young man doing my homework for me. As you can tell, I really didn't like school too much.

However, I did have an artistic gift, and I drew many things. The other kids in school asked me to draw temporary tattoos on them. I enjoyed that, and had many friends from every kind of clique. My brother, sister, and I knew lot of people. We all hit the teenage years at the same time. As a teen I was demanding and selfish—the rebellion inside of me was so terribly strong. I would almost call my behavior self-destructive at times or unruly. I had great gifts inside of me— people skills, artistry, and I loved to dance. I was voted best dancer in the yearbook for my hip-hop style of dancing. I inherited rhythm from my mother. Oh, and if there was a party, I could gather so many people to make it large. **My talents needed a good direction, but I had no moral core to help harness me in.**

One day, while my dad was homeless and waiting for his drug connection, a man appeared to him. He said, "God has a plan for you and it's not this. Your life is going to change." He turned around and the man had disappeared. My dad believes he had an encounter with angel. Minutes after his experience, another man approached him and invited him to live at a Christian men's home. He began the process of detoxing and learning about the Bible.

My family and I visited the church that ran the men's home. I remember the Pastor's daughter asking to hang out with me where I lived and to spend the night with us out there. I had this big "no" in my heart to not take her. I believe God had given me a warning and I didn't want to be the cause of ruining this girl. I ended up making an excuse to not take her. **I didn't understand anything at church during that time. I was still spiritually blind.**

At some point at around the age of sixteen, I made a friend named Nikki who took me for a week to her home. She was about five to six years older than I, and had kids that I babysat. I loved my friend. She was a biker chick who got saved. I received her outreach to me because I thought she was cool. She approached me about Jesus and took me to church and a seed was planted in my heart that day—although I hadn't yet received the Lord. Later on, that planted seed in my heart helped save my life. **Nikki's time with me had an impact, even though I hadn't changed yet. That seed (God's**

Word) was planted on good ground. This planted seed by Nikki wasn't wasted. Faith is believing, even when you cannot see the end result. The seed was in the ground, and God himself would make it grow.

My poor mom had her hands full with both Patrick and me; we were one and the same. We were loud, popular, and artsy. I would take my mom's marijuana plants and would smoke it junior high, I also cut school and would drink alcohol on occasion. Patricia, the middle child, was always a good student and worker. She seemed to have more control of her outward actions. She didn't give Mom too much trouble growing up. For some reason, she always seemed distant and disconnected from our family.

My brother got a girl pregnant about the age of fourteen. This situation seemed hard on my mother because my brother was so young and naïve. **The child later grew up to be a fine young man who served our country in the military. He is a blessing in our lives. No child is ever a mistake; every one is a gift from God.**

Then, that same year something terrible happened. Mom let Patrick go out trick or treating with his buddies without parental supervision, while my sister and I were out with our friends. I don't know why or what happened, but my brother and his friends did something terribly wrong and beat an innocent kid almost to death. The young man lived, but he had severe brain damage.

My mom went to apologize to the parents of that young man. She was not about to bail out Patrick, and she told the judge to let him do the time. Consequently, he went to juvenile hall for a few years and paid his own financial restitution to the young man. My brother, with my mom's help, still ended up graduating from high school.

At about sixteen and a half, I met a handsome young man with tan skin, blonde hair, and blue eyes—my first serious boyfriend. His name was Rick. This ended up being a destructive relationship. Having no proper male role model, I clung to him, even though he wasn't nice to me. Rick always accused me of having wandering eyes and became violent with me. I thought this abusive relationship was love. **I think back and wish someone would have reached out to me as I do now, to young women.**

During this time, my dad was still in the men's home. My dad had an advisor—a relative of his—someone to whom he would tell everything. That "Christian" woman said horrible things about me to my dad. In the past, when I was much younger, this relative had been cruel to me. She had accused me of stealing from her daughter, and would treat me harshly. I had never once even thought of doing such a thing. This family member never once invited me to church or poured out any Christian love toward me. It puzzled me why she seemed to dislike me so much when she never had a conversation with me or reached out to me. My dad had trusted her and told her how he felt about me and my lifestyle.

Later, a man of God—a prophet and leader at the men's home— met with my dad and his advisor. After the initial conversation, the man of God talked alone with my dad. This prophet gave my dad encouragement regarding his unrest about my lifestyle. He told my dad that he highly doubted the salvation of my dad's "Christian" advisor because of the cruel way she had talked about me. He went on to say, "Your daughter—you have no idea what she will become. She will go through many trials, but she will be great in the eyes of The Lord."

My dad told me about this, many years later.

From my teenage years to adulthood, I painted windows during Christmastime. This talent helped me out financially. I would paint snowmen, Santa, or whatever the customer wanted. Art had a way of taking me away from my problems, and being creative with art always had a positive effect on me. My mom told me that ever since she could remember, I always drew the Peanut characters.

The older that I got, the more I became the center of attention in my family because of the trouble that I caused. I would push my mom's buttons begging her to let me stay out late, and I had bad grades. I was also sick of my dad trying to "lay down the law" after being in and out of rehab and jail so many times. I was angry, and felt he did not deserve my respect. Both my parents wanted me to go to the juvenile hall but from what I understood I hadn't committed a crime to put me there. Instead, they took me to a halfway house for youth. The next day my parents and I had to go to counseling.

When the counselor got to me, I expressed my deep hurts a little bit. When I shared my frustration with my father going in and out of prison and using heroin, he lunged at me and scared that poor counselor. My parents ended up taking me home. My dad went back in the county jail after that for reasons I don't remember.

My mom tried so hard to get me to go to school, but I wouldn't listen. For one thing, I wanted to see my boyfriend and didn't care what anyone thought. I was very bossy, and if my sister was on the phone, I would demand she get off whenever I wanted. It was so wrong. I was selfish living how I wanted to live, and no one could have told me any different. During this time, I would go to my Christian neighbor Blanche's house to call my boyfriend. I don't know how to explain what I felt at her house, but I had similar feelings to what I'd had at Mrs. Morrow's house, years before. Blanche's house had a comforting peace that I didn't want to leave, and I would just sit there as I had done at Mrs. Morrow's. I had a lot of unanswered questions, but didn't even know what to ask for—I just liked to be in that peaceful presence. **I now know, I felt the presence of the Lord in their homes, and I unknowingly I soaked it in.**

Chapter 2

Psalm 30:11 (NIV)

> *"You turned my wailing into dancing; you removed my sackcloth and clothed me with joy,"*

Jeremiah 30:17 (NIV)

> *"'But I will restore you to health and heal your wounds,' declares the LORD, 'because you are called an outcast, Zion for whom no one cares.'"*

Hurting people can hurt people. But those who have been healed by Jesus, become healers in the name of the Lord. That's what my prayer is for those who have suffered from abuse.

At about age seventeen, I had a real meltdown. The same person who molested me when I was younger, molested my younger relatives.

This brought up bad memories for me that really hurt. When this happened to these kids too, I felt that I had to speak up to protect them.

So often when someone has been abused themselves, they hurt another in the same way. It's a mad cycle. I felt both upset and angry—not necessarily because of what happened to me with sexual abuse but, because for many years, I couldn't talk about it. **I believe to this day that there are many children who endure and/ or have endured sexual abuse and stay silent, in fear that no one will believe them. There have even been some parents and relatives that have ignored their cries for help and shoved the matter under the rug. Also, children have been told not to talk about it, forcing them into silent suffering.**

The predator gets away with what they have done if no one will face the truth. If nothing is done more than likely they will commit the act again, making more victims along the way.

A predator takes away a child's self-worth, intimidates them, and makes them feel dirty. Their young minds were never intended to handle such a big problem. The child may feel like it's somehow their fault the abuse happened. I was told I "wanted it." I am sure these very words have been told to many children. So they are silenced. They put the horror into the private archives of their minds—all boxed up.

I completely forgave those who hurt me and no longer feel anger or resentment for them. I sincerely love and care for their families and empathize with their pain.

As parents, we must do our best to protect our kids, teach them about God's forgiveness and give them the tools to help protect them from those who may want to harm them. I feel for those of you who have endured molestation or rape. My heart breaks every time I hear another story about sexual abuse. Please know that Christ can heal every wrong touch, along with the shame and anger toward the one who wronged you and those who didn't believe you. My parents believed me, but they didn't know how to heal me — only our Savior can do that.

When I turned eighteen I moved out with my boyfriend, Rick. We moved about twenty minutes away from my home town. Because of my immaturity, I didn't know better. While living with him, he pointed some kind of gun at me and hit me. I felt insecure and thought I would die without him in my life, but living together lasted no more than three months. It was over. He moved out and then I did. Convinced by my parents, I moved to Oregon with a relative. I tried calling Mom, but Dad had control of the phone. Although I asked for her, I would have to listen to my dad tell me everything wrong with me, and he wouldn't let me talk to her if I defended myself even a little to him. I wanted my mom. I was such a confused and hurt young lady, and I couldn't even say hi to my mom. I realize now that Mom allowed him to have that much control over her life, even though her child needed her. My aunt did get on the phone, upset with my dad because she felt he was wrong, but it didn't help me. I needed Mom's guidance. I didn't respect my dad because of his addiction and the way he went in and out of the prison system and our family's lives. Life seemed hopeless to me and I was so unhappy.

I remember while working at a store in Oregon, a couple came in talking about the Lord. I kid you not, something in me wanted to say, "Please take me with you." I really believe God was preparing my heart. I always had a respect for Christians but didn't know many. Christians, I thought, were like a nationality and you had to be born into it. I admired them and I could literally tell a difference when someone had Jesus. They had a drawing effect. At this point in my life, I had seen only a couple of believers and they all had the same sort of "light" on them. Later in my life I would come to understand.

During these days I felt so unstable in my emotions. My heart was broken and I was crying out inside but no one could hear it. It seemed like no one cared. But God in heaven who knows all things was stepping in and I didn't even know it yet. Looking back, I see all the times I could have died but the Lord intervened. I knew he was real but I didn't know how to reach him.

Chapter 3

Romans 1:20 (NLT)

> *"For ever since the world was created, people have seen the earth and sky. Through everything God made, they can clearly see his invisible qualities— his eternal power and divine nature. So they have no excuse for not knowing God."*

Psalm 27:10 (NKJV)

> *"When my father and my mother forsake me, then the Lord will take care of me."*

I stayed there in Oregon with my aunt. I liked her and she was good to me. My first cousin—about the same age as I—stayed there as well. I loved them, but I longed to come back to California. Deep inside I wanted to see Rick again.

Obviously, I lacked self-esteem, wanting to hold on to such a no-good person. After my own parents' rejection, I wanted to belong to somebody. At the time I thought that somebody was Rick. I wanted love so badly. I called my Aunt Liz, who lived in California, and she told me I could come live with her and her boyfriend. So I left on the bus to California.

I lived with my aunt a couple of months, then my aunt explained she and her boyfriend needed space. I had to leave Aunt Liz's house and I had nowhere to live. I moved from house to house, leaving my belongings in my broken-down car. One night I saw my ex-boyfriend Rick with another girl and I felt devastated. She and I had gone to the same school and were, at one time, friends. Later on when I saw her, I got in a fight with her, and then apologized because I didn't want her to press charges on me. **It seems so childish now, but during that time my actions were reckless**. It was as if I lost everything I ever loved. I felt worthless and unwanted. It was as if no one valued me and I don't think I even liked myself. No one could fix what was wrong with my heart.

I had put all my hope in a man, and in the end, it failed me. Rick not wanting me made me feel worthless, but I had given him that power. Ending my life seemed like the only way out from the despair I felt in my life.

That night in my hopelessness and thoughts of suicide, I went out on a search and stopped at the Catholic Church in our city. The church had a tall stairway outside, and I sat down on a step and cried out to the God I didn't know. Anguished in spirit and desperate for peace, I said, "Everything I see speaks to me that you must be real, but I don't know you! Even the stars speak to me, so you must be real." Still feeling suicidal, I drove to my mom's house that night.

My dad was gone again—I think back in prison. I drove up to the driveway and said, "Mama, please let me come home," My mom told me, "No, you can't come back." I cried out, tired and very weary from life, "Mama please, I feel like killing myself," She told me again, "No, you can't come back." Then, my little brother said to my mom, "If she kills herself, I will never forgive you!" That got my mom's attention, and she let me in. I slept soundly that night, happy to have a home. I had tired of trying to find somewhere to sleep; tired of running here and there and burdening people. I obeyed my mom, helped with the chores, kept my curfew, and got a job.

Chapter 4

Psalm 139:16 (NLT)

*"You saw me before I was born. Every day of my life
was recorded in your book. Every moment was laid
out before a single day had passed."*

Icouldn't wait to see my best friend Darla, who now had small children. She had married a nice man named Tom, and I was so happy she chose a good person. They had two cute kids. After our visit, Tom dropped me off at my friend's house near the high school. As I got out of the car, here came Louis—an old acquaintance—walking toward us. He said hello to Tom—they were friends from school. Louis looked so handsome, easy on the eyes for sure. I had first seen him at a pizza parlor when I was sixteen years old. At the time, he had stood up out of his chair surrounded by his soccer buddies to smile at me and stare a while. I thought to myself, "He's *too* good looking. He's probably a player." Later, when I saw him around town he always said hello to me. So after Louis spoke to Tom he turned his attention to me, he said "Hi, Lisa." I said, "Hi." He said, "So you want to go out tonight?" I said sure. I liked him immediately.

I don't think either of us felt very serious about each other yet. I still had feelings for Rick. One day I got a phone call from Rick telling me, "Louis cheated on you with this girl and she wants to be with me tonight. But if you'll come and let me pick you up I would rather be with you instead." I said, "Sure, I'll meet you!" I had no intention of going and I let him wait for nothing. I wanted to get him back for being such a loser.

I was permanently done with him this time. That day I decided I wanted to be serious with Louis. Louis made me laugh, he admired my mother, and he always told me I was beautiful. He had strikingly handsome features, and large, muscular arms. He was Latin, darker than I and had beautiful brown eyes and long lashes. Louis was very popular and athletic. Just about every woman I knew had a crush on him. We danced well together and had a lot in common. He took care of me; he bought me things and helped me buy a car. I fell in love with him. Louis and I both had jobs; we worked out a lot and had fun together.

One negative, however, was how we often partied together using cocaine, meth, and alcohol. Partying was a blast at night, but the next day I would pay with a hangover and coming down from the drugs, both mentally and physically. Sin is fun for a short season, but it's a trick the enemy uses to try to take you out. I made plenty of mistakes during that time in my life. I felt fat all the time. Although quite skinny, I looked for ways to lose weight, and started with diet pills and laxatives. Then I went onto binging and purging (anorexia and bulimia). I was slim from working out with Louis at the gym, but it wasn't good enough for me. I was really messed up mentally. I had an unrealistic expectation of myself to look like the very skinny girls I knew. I tried to go against my natural body type. I went into the shower and put my finger down my throat every day, a few times a day. The acid eventually took some of the enamel off my teeth. How fortunate, that I didn't die from this.

Chapter 5

Psalm 138:7 (NLT)

> *"Though I am surrounded by troubles, you will protect me from the anger of my enemies. You reach out your hand, and the power of your right hand saves me."*

Psalms 91:11–12 (NLT)

> *"For he will order his angel to protect you wherever you go. They will hold you up with their hands so you won't even hurt your foot on a stone."*

During the time that Louis and I dated something happened to my family. My mom, my brother Patrick, his best friend, Cliff, and Patrick's girlfriend, Bonnie, went fishing late at night on a bridge over the ocean. Louis and I had planned to go with them—he had just bought a gun and he would have brought it for protection.

For some reason we couldn't make it. The group fished along with a few other people off of a dark and long pier. They set up poles and chairs and had dressed warmly. Cliff, a Caucasian boy, had on a black bandana. Around midnight, my mom told me she started hearing a roar of voices coming out of the dark and that she had an eerie feeling. As the voices got louder and closer, Mom noticed lots of Latino teenage boys, like phantoms in the night, coming from the darkness. She had great fear as they came closer with beer in their hands. My family and their group tried to ignore them. These young men, dressed in red, were obviously gang affiliated, as was shown by the color they wore. They asked Cliff if he was wearing a blue rag, their rival's colors, and Cliff told them he wasn't. Cliff never gang-banged in his life, but this group was looking for trouble. At least thirty of them got loud with my brother and Cliff. One picked up a chair and beat Cliff with it. Others lifted my brother in the air to throw him into the water—and he didn't know how to swim!

Just then, my mom screamed out, "God, please help us!" As soon as she said that, they let go of him and left. My mom told me later that she felt the evilness leave when they left. God protected my family from death that night.

The Lord knew my mom would one day give her heart to him. When she cried out to God, He scattered and confused the enemy.

Chapter 6

Job 33:28 (NLT)

"God rescued me from the grave, and now my life is filled with light."

Psalm 18:6 (NIV)

"In my distress I called to the LORD; I cried to my God for help. From his temple he heard my voice; my cry came before him, into his ears."

When I was about to turn twenty-one, Louis told me that he didn't want me going out to bars with friends and that he wanted to marry me. So, we got engaged. He bought me a pretty ring, and we moved in together and started planning our wedding. We were married in 1994 at a little chapel in Reno, Nevada.

I loved Louis so much. We both made a decision to stay sober and drug-free at our wedding.

Everyone had great fun at the wedding. Even my Great Grandmother, who was from Puerto Rico, came to celebrate with us. Louis looked handsome in a white tuxedo with a little black bow tie; I wore my hair up with a mermaid-style beaded wedding dress. I worked with children in the schools at the time and two of the little girls who went to the school, were my pretty little flower girls. We had some help to make the event happen. My godmother Tia helped pay for a lot of things, including my dress and pictures. I chose royal blue as my accent color and my mother made flower bouquets for my bridesmaids and for me.

Louis and I went to Texas for our honeymoon where his dad and uncle owned a little penthouse by the ocean. His family stayed with us during our honeymoon. We couldn't afford anything else, but Louis and I tried to make the most of it. The highlight of the entire vacation was when I met his Aunt Bertha. What a wonderful lady — small, cute, and a great fisherwoman. We went out on a jetty and fished. I was so excited when I caught a Ribbon Fish on the Gulf of Mexico! I didn't leave the dock until 2:00 a.m. and I remember poor Louis saying, "Can we go now babe?" Finally, I came in. Although the rest of the honeymoon went okay, I couldn't wait to come back home to California.

About a month after our marriage, Louis had an invitation to his good friend's wedding. He wouldn't allow me to go and wanted to go with his mother. I felt terribly hurt and couldn't understand why on earth he wouldn't take me, his wife. I found out the location of the reception and, after the wedding, went there anyway. His mom had left at that point had gone home. Louis did not welcome me when I arrived, and he treated me with no respect that night.

Louis had been drinking and flirting with an indecently dressed young woman. Right in front of me, he told her to come and sit on his lap. He even spit on me in front of people. He said he didn't like being married, and it absolutely broke my heart. I felt rejected and I really wanted to beat up the girl who had dressed indecently. I blamed her for Louis' actions, so I asked her to come speak with me in the corner. She asked me if I was going to hurt her. I had planned to, but Louis's friend (thank God), stopped me. What a terrible night. I felt brokenhearted.

I begged Louis to come home, and he finally said he would. I had driven our car and we needed to go pick it up. So he borrowed his friend's truck and we drove out to get our car. Louis proceeded to get in his friend's truck and drive off. I would follow him back to the reception in our car. All of a sudden, he went onto the freeway, speeding, and tried to lose me. I couldn't catch up and slowed down to average speed. While driving, I felt so empty and lost inside my soul. My parents, my new husband, and I, all had major problems. I heard a voice while driving (just as sure as if I were talking out loud to you) say to me, "Kill yourself; run off a cliff. Go into a wall, nobody loves you!" I cried out to the unknown God, "If you are real, please help me!" Right then, I had a vision. I saw people with their hands lifted worshipping God in church. In my desperation I said to God, "I want that!"

Soon after this experience, I went back to the church my friend Nikki had taken me to, years before. I told God, "All my love, that a man spit on, I give to you." All of a sudden, my eyes were opened. I knew deep down inside that Christ himself removed the blinders and now I could see. My Jesus was now real and attainable to me. Oh, the love I had for Him. I never did drugs again, and started to wean myself off of alcohol. I started reading the Bible and praying for Louis. I said to God, "I'm going back and I'm going to make my marriage work."

Chapter 7

Psalm 127:3 (NIV)

"Children are a heritage from the LORD, offspring a reward from him."

Although I had a dysfunctional marriage, I loved Louis, regardless of his actions, and I prayed to God that I would become pregnant. Right or wrong in the eyes of other people, I wanted to be a mother and to share my love with my own child. It was my heart's desire.

A year after I married, I found out I was pregnant with my daughter, Lani—an answer my prayers. A disgruntled Louis panicked about money, and he talked about an abortion. I refused and told him, "No way." His mom called me after finding out and had the nerve to say, "You trapped my son."

Soon after finding out about my pregnancy, I started bleeding and went to an urgent care center. I'd never heard of the doctor who examined me. He proceeded to tell me that I was losing the baby, and that "these things just happen." I looked at him and said, "I will not lose this baby, doctor. God promised me this baby."

I ran into the bathroom, closed the door and began to pray. The nurse knocked on the door and said, "Honey, these things sometimes happen. You will have another child," but I would not answer her. I was praying and I knew God would listen to me. I called my mother and I asked her to take me to a hospital. She picked me up and we went. The hospital had more modern equipment and a doctor ordered an ultrasound that confirmed the baby looked completely fine. God once again had come through for me and my baby was okay.

I had such a good pregnancy. I loved every kick, I loved getting bigger, and I loved eating whatever I wanted. I enjoyed being pregnant. I prayed over my stomach all the time and I read the Bible to Lani while she lay in my womb. My mother gave me a wonderful baby shower. On her front window, I painted a stork with a little girl wrapped in cloth in its mouth. Amazingly, my daughter ended up looking much like the picture I painted. As people started showing up to the baby shower, we had to move the furniture out in the backyard to make room for everyone my mom invited. I felt blessed, realizing so many people loved me and my mother.

My husband Louis worked hard to provide for us and the soon-to-be baby. He treated me better at this point. One day, he bought tickets to see his favorite team—the Oakland Raiders—play a big home game. He marinated fillet mignon and had his beer ready in his ice chest. His friends planned to meet him at the stadium for a tailgate party. I remember Louis telling me, "Out of any day, don't have the baby today because tomorrow is the big game."

I said to him, "I will try not to have the baby today." I actually thought he was kind of cute though. He loved the Raiders so much.

That night my water broke (Sorry, Lou! I tried!), and we went to the hospital. Louis did have a good attitude, however, and I felt sorry for him, so I told him to go ahead and watch the game while I was in labor. And he did—right next to me. While I huffed and puffed, Louis watched his Raider game. Every now and then, I'd get a semi-concerned, "You okay, Babe?" and I'd respond sarcastically, "Oh yeah! I'm fine!" and then he'd go back to his game, not taking a hint. He was a die-hard Raider fan.

Soon, the time came. 6 lbs. 9 oz. Baby Lani had brown skin like her daddy, a lot of black hair, and pretty, almond-shaped, dark brown eyes. She was my "Lani Poo" and Louis nicknamed her "Boo." He acted proud and attentive to Lani, while smiling from ear to ear. I was so apprehensive about bringing her home, I cried couple of times. I had so much fear of breaking her. Lani was God's gift to me, and I would always protect her.

Every day I sang to Lani, and every night I prayed with her and sang worship songs. I also kept Christmas alive all year by singing Christmas songs to her and watching lots of taped Christmas cartoons. We kept Jesus in our hearts every day, my baby and I. My elderly neighbor once told me that she could hear me singing to my

baby and said it was so nice. She also mentioned how she heard me
cry and heard my husband yelling at me. True, he had started acting
up again. Over time, I noticed that he had the signs of someone who
did meth. Weird gestures, runny nose, insomnia, lack of appetite, and
an overall strange demeanor. I tried to confront him about it a few
times, but he said I was imagining things. But I had Lani and Jesus,
so my heart overflowed with love. I prayed every day for Louis.

**Addiction not only hurts the addict, but all those who love
them. It's a mad cycle of really good times and then a huge fall of
bad times. Just like the feeling of a roller coaster, huge turns, dips,
fears, and shock. I knew addiction my whole life, even though
I wasn't always the one with the addiction. When I got saved,
my eyes were really opened to the demonic world made available through addiction. Sometimes drugs are used for an introverted person to be the life of the party. Sometimes people with
mental health issues self-medicate. Some people haven't dealt
with things they are trying to forget about: a horrible childhood,
or other places where they feel like a failure in life. They use
drugs to forget. All of a sudden for whatever reason, you start,
then find you cannot stop. Addiction is now second nature to you.
You think about it all the time. And you're in a daily fight with
yourself about it. You seek out old friends who have the drugs
you need. Then you're in it again—the roller coaster. Jesus literally delivered me from addiction. Remember the Bible says that**

what you allow will overtake you. Take captive every thought that's not of God, as it says in the Bible, 2 Corinthians 10:5 (KJV)

"Casting down imaginations, and every high thing that exalteth itself against the knowledge of God, and bringing into captivity every thought to the obedience of Christ;"

One of the fruits of the spirit is self-control. You have a choice. The Bible says to CHOOSE life. You can say no. If you're struggling, ask for some help.

1 Corinthians 15:33 (NIV) says, "Do not be misled: "Bad company corrupts good character.""

Chapter 8

2 Corinthians 10:5 (NKJV)

"Casting down arguments and every high thing that exalts itself against the knowledge of God, bringing every thought into captivity to the obedience of Christ."

Genesis 2:23–24 (NIV)

"The man said, "This is now bone of my bones and flesh of my flesh; She shall be called 'woman,' for she was taken out of man."
"That is why a man leaves his father and mother and is united to his wife, and they become one flesh."

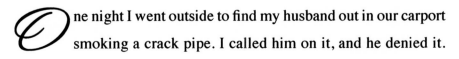 ne night I went outside to find my husband out in our carport smoking a crack pipe. I called him on it, and he denied it.

My heart just sank. This is one of worse addictions to kick. I really had no idea he was into this, I felt lied to. The next day I called my mother-in-law, Esperanza and left a message. When she called me back, I told her what he was up to and I asked her if we could have an intervention for Louis. I could foresee tragedy for him because of his drug use. She listened to me, and later on, I got a call from her sister Pam. She sounded angry with me. Pam told me she listened in on the three way call between Esperanza and I. Pam told me to never again bring up Louis' drug use to her sister, because it was stressing her out. She told me to leave Louis if I didn't like the way he acted. I said sorry to her and I wouldn't do it again. Somehow the blame was always put on me. Louis' family was in denial of his addiction, and I soon learned I couldn't trust them. And apparently, I couldn't even trust his family to do what was in Louis' best interest.

Once, in our little home, he hit me right in front of his mom. My baby was crying and Esperanza simply held her and watched silently without expression. This really bothered me; it felt like she hated me. She seemed to coddle and enable Louis but, in a sense, at that that time, I coddled him too. Rarely had anything physical happen to me through his hands, but he should have never done that to me. I should have stood up for myself. In a way, I married someone who behaved a lot like my father—something I swore I would never do. But that is in fact what I did. My heart still loved Louis, so I stayed. **I would not want anyone to go through what I did then.**

When Lani was eleven months old, we rented a house owned by Louis' dad. It was spacious and I ended up really liking it. Two years after Lani was born, I had a son named Louis Jr., and a year later I gave birth to our second son, Luke. Louis Jr. looked just like his dad and Luke resembled me.

My husband Louis had his good moments—the man could barbeque like no other. He would work all day in construction and come home to either his dinner that I would prepare, or he would barbeque. One of the mistakes I made as a young Christian were times when Louis would watch The 700 Club when I wasn't paying attention. When I caught him, here I'd come, a Junior Holy Spirit, "Oh Louis! Isn't that awesome about the Lord?" I would get overly excited and was probably more of a turnoff at times. **I should have let the Holy Spirit do His job. Being young in the Lord, I didn't realize that God could easily do the work without my help.** Louis was so excited about the Lord he even went to Promise Keepers. I was so happy for him. He went to Lani and Louis Jr.'s dedication at my church and he did try for a while. Once in a while he went to church with me. But soon, he would use drugs again and down we all went, suffering together. **The addict doesn't suffer alone; the loved ones of the addict suffer along with them.**

I had a terribly hard time with my mother-in-law, Esperanza, through my entire marriage. She was very hard on me—extremely critical—and wouldn't give me a chance. When I gave birth or went through labor she put me down because I had medicine for pain.

Louis told her once, "Mom, this is Lisa's day." Every time I turned around, Esperanza was trying to turn my husband against me. I wasn't good enough for her baby boy.

Esperanza would start fights between us and she seemed to enjoy it when we didn't get along. I did nothing good enough: my house-keeping, my cooking, and my parenting skills. Even I wasn't good enough. At times my husband and his mom would gang up against me, especially if he were either using or coming off of drugs. I felt sad, brokenhearted and always felt alone.

Louis would run to his mom's house to escape his responsibilities. I knew this behavior was wrong. The Bible says, "Leave your father and mother and cleave to your wife." This never happened for us. We had a roller-coaster marriage. My husband's dysfunctional family always pitted against someone or each other. I suffered a lot because of his family members' actions toward me—mainly from his mother and his brother, Joe.

I started praying deeply about things. God was teaching me how to pray for those who hurt me. I loved my husband so much. I would take off his work boots when he came home and I had joy serving him. **I felt that was my part and I still, to this day, am glad that I loved him so**. Never once did Louis wonder if I loved him. I showed him and told him often. I know that getting saved less than two months after we married was no easy thing for Louis because, at the time, he knew nothing about God.

Of course we had our moments of enjoying each other's company—usually when people left us alone and when he was sober. I did nice things for his friends and coworkers, such as making them cookies and special desserts. This always made Louis proud of me.

I also made things fun for my little ones. I had nice birthday parties with arts and crafts for the kids to do. Because of my artistry, I could paint their favorite characters on the windows. I enjoyed their childhood. They meant the world to me, and I was determined to keep our family together.

My husband's on again/off again drug addiction caused erratic things in our lives. I never knew when he would be nice Louis or cruel Louis. Anyone who has lived with an addict understands what I mean. My emotions went on this roller-coaster ride with him; one minute he was clean, then the next he would use drugs again. Then I would feel sad and disappointed again. When he was good, he was really good, and when he was bad, he was really bad. Our roles switched—I, took my mother's role and my husband, my father's—and his father.

The biggest difference between mine and my parents' situation: I had Jesus by my side, constantly helping me. I made good decisions because Christ was Lord over my life. Jesus' helping me through life gave me a whole new outlook. The things I found impossible to do before, became easier. Once we went to another Church (that was known for its powerful worship) to visit and, during worship, I felt the Lord consuming me with His holy presence. It was beautiful and oh, I loved it. I had my whole heart in that moment of worship. Louis looked at me in that moment and said, "What happening to you?" Later, he asked, "Where's my Lisa I married?"

I'm not sure why he felt so afraid but he looked and acted fearful of losing me. Of course that wasn't the truth at all; he was gaining a better Lisa. Because I loved God, I could love him so much better.

When it came to husband and wife time, I really loved him. I didn't neglect him in that way. He was my love, and daily I felt encouraged by God to stick it out.

Chapter 9

1 Corinthians 7:14 (NLT)

"For the Christian wife brings holiness to her marriage, and the Christian husband brings holiness to his marriage. Otherwise, your children would not be holy, but now they are holy."

1 Peter 4:4–5 (NLT)

"Of course, your former friends are surprised when you no longer plunge into the flood of wild and destructive things they do. So they slander you. But remember that they will have to face God, who will judge everyone, both the living and the dead."

Matthew 5:28 (NLT)

> *"But I say, anyone who even looks at a woman with lust has already committed adultery with her in his heart."*

During Thanksgiving and Christmas time, our families would come together. I enjoyed cooking and being a good hostess. Louis and I made menudo (a Mexican soup) for Christmas Eve and invited everyone. Friends and relatives would come over when they could.

I decorated my house every year, painting art on the front window and trimming the tree lavishly. I baked many delicious cookies of different kinds and everyone told me I should open up a bakery. My kids loved taking part in the cookie-making process.

When I cooked, and people liked my food, Louis showed his pride in me. It brought me great joy to be his wife.

Louis didn't work much in the winter, so every year I went out and painted Christmas art on merchants' windows for extra money. The skill I learned as a teenager helped us through those rough months. I also babysat all week to help with our grocery bill. This enabled me to stay home and raise my babies while still helping bring in income. I so enjoyed staying at home with my babies.

I sang to every one of my kids at night and I taught them to pray to the Lord, and watched a lot of Christian cartoons with my children as they grew up. I bought all the Christian VHS tapes such as, Veggie Tales and Bible Man. I taught my babies Christian Songs and Bible scriptures. They had the Lord's word in their little hearts. My brilliant daughter Lani, started reading scriptures at age three with help from her mama—she was the only one of my children who started reading so young. **Till this day she excels in English.**

The scriptures I read during this time breathed life and strength into my being. God himself taught me. The scripture says, "But when the Father sends the Advocate as my representative—that is, the Holy Spirit—he will teach you everything and will remind you of everything I have told you." -John 14:26. God called me away from people. I no longer enjoyed my time at gatherings where some family and friends drank heavily and smoked pot. It really started to grieve my spirit.

Sitting in my chair one night while reading the Bible, I came across a scripture that seemed to put everything into perspective. "Of course, your former friends are very surprised when you no longer join them in the wicked things they do, and they say evil things about you. But just remember that they will have to face God, who will judge everyone, both the living and the dead." 1 Peter 4:4–5. I then heard God speak to my heart, "Come away with me and I will give you new friends; ones that will pray for you."

I happily stayed home with my babies, although lonely for Louis while he went out partying on the weekends. It broke my heart when I found a glass pipe and old plastic bags used for meth with residue.

I also would find pornography videos and magazines. It made die inside and hurt me badly. I had the feeling that I wasn't enough for my husband. It felt as if we lived two different lives. But he still meant a lot to me, and I continued to be a good wife and mom. I couldn't wait for church to come on Sundays.

At times, my husband had issues with getting along with his older, controlling brother, Joe. Louis reacted passively and seemed to always give in to Joe's demands.

Louis also struggled with lust. His wandering eyes became an issue especially when he was on or coming off of drugs. I felt inadequate; I felt like his wandering eyes reflected on and caused me embarrassment. He shared with me about how much his dad hurt his mom with that issue of lust as he grew up. My husband truly struggled, but I always forgave him. Once I got so angry that I took a hammer to videos I found with pornography on them. His ugly addiction upset me so, that it felt like he was having an affair.

As I said, Louis really didn't work in construction very much in the winter. Our funds got low. One day Louis told me he would run to store to get a few things. We needed diapers, food and formula. He filled a basket with diapers, formula and food and tried to walk out of the store with it. Louis was caught. He had a warning from the judge not to steal again. A few months later, he did the same crime again. He filled a basket with baby food, diapers and milk. Again he was caught and, this time, went to jail. I must have been twenty-six at that time. I started fasting and praying and wouldn't allow anyone to walk in my house speaking anything but faith for him. He could get a fifteen month sentence.

With our home in jeopardy, I prayed determinedly. My husband's freedom was at stake, and I would not sit back and let the enemy have his way in our lives. I sought God with all my heart, believing for a breakthrough. I remember certain family members walking in our home during that time with comments like, "Well you know he's probably going to prison!" or "What are you going to do? You're probably going to have to move!" I responded optimistically, I fervently prayed to God, a persistent widow kind of prayer (Luke 18:1–8). I felt as if I held onto the hem of Jesus's robe and I would not let go. My heart and mind were fixed.

I started asking the Lord (knowing Louis might face prison time) to please allow me to run into the judge before court started.

One morning I woke up, went down to the courthouse early and just that happened. I ran into the judge. "Please sir, have mercy," I told him. "What did you do?" he asked, I told him, "It's not me, but my husband. He stole a basket of food from a grocery store and he is the sole provider for me and our family. Please give him a chance!" The judge said, "Alright, I'll tell you what. When court starts, you stand up and ask if you can speak. I must be on record." I said, "Thank you, sir."

When Esperanza and I went to court, a handsome Latin attorney seduced me with his eyes and stared at me, smiling the whole time I sat in the courtroom. He was so obvious, that my mother-in-law, who sat next to me, said, "Look at him, he can't get his eyes off of you! He's so handsome."

I said, "Esperanza, I love your son!" **(I have a reason to bring up this attorney because I will see him again years later.)**

The judge threw the book at him—a prior conviction of the same crime in one year meant fifteen months in prison. My husband's face hung low as if he had given up. I stood up quickly and addressed the judge, "Sir, can I please speak on behalf of my husband?" The judge responded by telling me, "Mrs. Moreno, when you came to me this morning I didn't know he had previously done the same crime. He is a danger to the community. He is going away for a long time."

I then prayed in my heart, "Lord, you say in your word, "Do not worry about what you are going to say for I will give you the words at the appropriate time."" I lifted my head and could feel boldness in my spirit. "Sir, yes my husband is guilty and he should be punished for what he did; but think about what he stole. Diapers, formula, and milk—all things for his kids. He didn't have beer and cigarettes. I believe he is sorry for what he has done. I am a Christian and I believe that's the way he is headed."

The judge shook his head speechless for a few minutes and said, "Mrs. Moreno, you smack him on the head and tell him if he comes in my courtroom again he is going to be doing prison time."

"Yes sir, I will," I replied.

I heard someone in the audience of the courtroom say with a shout, "Here, Here!" and the audience started clapping.

When I finished, my mother-in-law turned to me and said, "I'm so proud of you!"

When Louis got out of jail, he told me how proud I made him and that the guys behind bars all had hope after I spoke up. They said to Louis, "Your wife is a warrior, a straight up warrior!"

I started really hearing God's voice and feeling so much love for people. I went into stores and prayed for complete strangers and God set it all up. I started evangelizing wherever I went before I even knew what the word evangelist meant. I would tell people everywhere all about Jesus and all that he had done for me. Sharing the gospel of Christ made me feel fulfilled; I loved being used for His kingdom.

Chapter 10

Joel 2:28 (NLT)

> *"Then, after doing all those things, I will pour out my Spirit upon all people. Your sons and daughters will prophesy. Your old men will dream dreams, and your young men will see visions."*

I had two large gardens and I grew many vegetables and herbs. I know it may sound silly, but I would open up my back windows and face the speakers filled with worship music toward my garden. God blessed my garden and it flourished. Many times, Mom would come over to my house and help me with the garden and other things. She would do most of the gardening; a real worker that one. I always said she had a Midas touch.

I started reaching out to my elderly neighbors and went to their Christmas parties and visited them. I gave them a lot of my garden vegetables and spoke often about Jesus.

There was an elderly neighbor couple that lived across the street from me. The woman went to a church with different views on who Jesus was, her husband was a Christian. They wouldn't get along because of their different beliefs. For some reason my neighbor, who lived across the street, adored me and my kids, her name was Lana. I had a lot of love for her and checked up on her regularly because of her ill health. I always cried with her when she felt sad.

One day, as I did my dishes, I suddenly I had a vision: I saw Lana on the ground outside, full of blood, calling my name. I abruptly dropped my dish and ran to the front of my home. There she lay on the ground, in a pool of blood, screaming my name.

I cried when I saw her and said, "Lana, what happened?"

"Lisa," she said, "I was calling your name."

I told her that I'd had a vision of her from the Lord Jesus and that was what brought me to her. She understood and received so well from me. I picked her up, carried her into her house and got help.

Many years later, Lana became blind and we talked and prayed together. I had the chance to pray the salvation prayer with her and soon after, she passed away. Bless the Lord that I ever even knew this wonderful lady; I loved her.

My husband's continued drug abuse made me feel increasingly distant from him. We grew to have less and less in common. I really needed a friend to talk to and my old ones didn't cut it for me anymore.

God did send me a friend. I met Mary at the church I attended at the time and we quickly made a connection. Mary was near my age and a fine example of a Christian woman. She came from a family of Christian people, and I admired her so much. Mary was so sweet to my children and me. Together, we did aerobics, prayed nearly every day, and had play dates with our children. We became very close. She helped me by teaching me the ropes of homeschooling and gave me life lessons on child rearing. Mary was a good influence on me. She was a dedicated mom and wife, and loved Jesus so much. As a young Christian, I really gleaned from her example. I took pride in my Christian friend; she was like a sister to me.

During this time, God transformed me. Still a new believer, I had not yet completely matured in the Lord. Fully aware of my imperfections, I'm sure I didn't do and say all the right things, but I hungered for God and had lots of faith. I believed, as I still believe, that God will do anything His children ask if it's according to his plan.

Once when Mary and I prayed, we asked God to provide what I needed from the store. I asked God specifically for corned beef and cabbage, penne pasta, tuna and peas to make certain dishes for my family.

That same day, a woman named May came to my door and said, "Before you open this bag, I have to tell you what happened."

May explained to me that while she visited with her dad at the retirement home, she held her head and told her father, "I can't get this little girl out of my mind. God keeps telling me she's praying for food."

He told her, "Well then, go get it!"

May went to the grocery store and as she walked down each aisle, she said God would direct her. He even directed her to the right kind of pasta. When she picked up spaghetti noodles, God told her, "Not that one, she wants that one," referring to the penne pasta.

May explained that she felt like God told her every item she should buy. When she said, "I don't think she'll like this, God." He responded, "That's what she's praying for."

After she told me what had happened, I opened it up the grocery bag and, sure enough, saw exactly the items I prayed for. We both cried because of God's goodness to us. She felt just as blessed as I to hear from The Lord. I learned a great deal in these years about God providing.

During that time in my life, I had stopped sleeping in the same bed with Louis because of my frustration with him and his lifestyle. One night, I heard the voice of the Lord while I lay sleeping with my children. God said, "Wake up, wake up," and I replied, "Yes, Lord." "Satan is trying to cause division in your marriage." Again I replied, "Yes, Lord." The Holy Spirit in me knew what God had meant. I dropped to my knees and prayed to Him. God encouraged intimacy with my husband again. I followed God's plan.

I prayed for my mom to be set free from her dependence on marijuana and I also prayed for her to come to The Lord. My mom did acknowledge God, but she hadn't fully surrendered.

One day, while I prayed, the Lord gave me a message for her. I told her, "Mama, God came to me and said because you will not surrender, something drastic is going to happen to you." One month later, His words came to pass.

A few days before Easter while my friend Mary and I prayed, I suddenly felt inclined by God to pray for Mom. I said, "I pray now for my mom, safety in her car—to and from her destination. I pray Psalm 91 over her, God that you would give your angels charge over her."

At the same moment we prayed, Mom was in a head-on collision.

The hospital called me and asked, "Are you Lisa?"

When I replied, "Yes, I am," they told me, "Your mom has been in a car accident." "What?" I said, "How bad is it?"

The nurse told me she couldn't explain over the phone, but that I needed to come down quickly because my mom kept calling my name.

Mom had gone shopping that morning to buy Easter cards and some things for my kids. She had just left the residence where she housecleaned, and out of nowhere, a car hit her. Two high school girls had raced down the street, going 55 in a 25 mile-an-hour zone, and one of the girls suddenly crossed a double yellow line and hit my mom head on. This made her little car fly into the air, and land on a parked car across the street. The force smashed her in the car, and caused mom to lose consciousness. It took the Jaws of Life to release my mother from her vehicle. A helicopter took her to a trauma center at an excellent hospital.

Mom's injuries included a broken hip bone, and her pelvic bone had shattered beyond repair. She had lacerations everywhere and lay in traction for four days. A doctor drilled a bar through her knee until it was time for surgery fourteen days later. My mom endured excruciating pain and she stayed in bed for six months. While Mom was in the hospital, Dad and I hired an attorney to take on her case.

The young woman who hit my mom had an umbrella insurance coverage, which was good for Mom's case. The young women's attorneys and my mom's came to an agreement out of court. It so happened when Mom met with their insurance adjuster that he was retiring and it was his last day working for the company. In a whim, he approved a great amount of money to be granted to my mother.

Mom told me she feared going home because she knew the temptation of marijuana awaited her. I prayed that she would resist the temptation and not go back to her old ways.

One day as I was prayed for someone to help mentor me, God gave me two signs that directed me to that person. My friend Mary told me about a woman at her church, named Carol, who held a Bible study at her house in my city. Then, another friend of mine who worked with Carol asked me if I knew a woman named Carol. She told, "Carol loves the Lord and is a strong Christian lady."

I said, "What? That's so crazy! My friend just mentioned her to me too."

I took these as signs that I needed to go to Carol's Bible study, which I had been hearing so much about.

Carol and her husband, Matthew, lived in a pretty home on the nicer side of town. I brought friends and family with me to Carol's house for Bible study. Carol and her husband Matthew didn't mind, so I kept inviting more people every Monday night. I had a great time. I was finally around a group of people who loved Jesus like me. Carol, Matthew and the others who attended were mature in age, and had a relationship with the Lord longer than I, and I honored that. Their house felt warm and inviting, and they shared love.

Carol and Matthew welcomed my friends and family into their home. I brought Louis a few times to the Bible study, but more often took my kids.

I will never forget when Carol brought the prettiest cookies to my home for Christmas. I really liked this woman. She was a few years older than my mom, and she had the gift of intercession, which I respected. I learned from this couple the importance of praying in unity with other Christians. It was good for my family and me for a time.

I was the youngest adult there during that time, except for the friends I would bring to the meetings. I was so excited to be around other Christians at these meetings. I also brought lots of new people to the weekly meetings. They needed to know God and the Bible. My desire was that many people would come to know Jesus.

Chapter 11

Titus 1:7–14 (NIV)

"Since an overseer manages God's household, he must be blameless—not overbearing, not quick-tempered, not given to drunkenness, not violent, not pursuing dishonest gain. 8 Rather, he must be hospitable, one who loves what is good, who is self-controlled, upright, holy and disciplined. He must hold firmly to the trustworthy message as it has been taught, so that he can encourage others by sound doctrine and refute those who oppose it."

1 Timothy 4:12 (NLT)

"Don't let anyone think less of you because you are young. Be an example to all believers in what you

say, in the way you live, in your love, your faith, and your purity."

During these years God started using my life outside the church walls and outside of bible study. I would go out to stores, doctors' offices, wherever I went the Lord would use me to encourage people, especially those who did not know Him. In this, I could be myself and no one but God could tell me what to do, because His spirit led me.

I continued to live for God, and my influence on those around me grew. Some people received the Lord's message, while others couldn't and didn't receive from me. I remember my mother-in-law, Esperanza, mentioning that I used to do drugs with her sons, Joe and Louis. My answer to her was, "Yes, it's true. But that Lisa is dead and gone; I'm a new creation."

2 Corinthians 5:17 (NLT)

"This means that anyone who belongs to Christ has become a new person. The old life is gone; a new life has begun!"

My mother did end up coming home from the hospital, and I had a prompting in my heart to make every effort to go on my first missionary field trip. Louis didn't mind if I went; I think he wanted some freedom. Since he would be working while I was gone, he couldn't watch the kids. The only other person I trusted to watch them was Mom, but she started treating me badly and acted mean-spirited towards me. When I asked if she would watch my kids, she refused. I continued to love her, in spite of her indifference. As my mentor, Carol helped me pray me through it. I had a friend in her and in Mary. God had covered me in prayer and I rode on the wings of faith.

The time soon approached for the missionary field trip, but I had no babysitter for my three children. I believed that since God told me to go, he would provide a way. I waited and prayed.

Esperanza started to act up, Mom treated me badly, and my husband and I did not get along. I felt the warfare; my body sickened with fever, and I was sleepless. I prayed in my room and said to Jesus, "I'm so sick, Lord help me."

I heard the Lord speak to my heart, "Get up and dance," he said.

I replied, "I can't dance, Lord. I'm so sick."

The Lord repeated himself, "Get up and dance."

I got up, put on worship music, and danced. I danced until my joy came back, and then I had peace, focusing no longer on my physical sickness or on others, but instead, on my Jesus.

I sat by the door and waited for God.

God came through; my mom called me and said, "Go to Mexico. I'll watch the kids." She said, "If you don't go, I'll be mad." My mom always treated the kids with love.

Mom drove me to the church where I met the mission's team. Once I got on the bus, my fever broke, and my sickness left.

I went to Mexico, and had the amazing opportunity to serve. Our team went to orphanages, fed the poor, and clothed them. In the evening we went to church services and ministered to people. The pastor with us gave a good message, and then we had the opportunity to pray for people. It brought them great hope.

I called and checked up on my children frequently, and they were fine. Although Mom sounded angry with me, God used her as a safe and reliable babysitter for my children. My kids loved their grandma.

When I came back home, my mom went back to her home, called me on the phone, and screamed, "Because of you, I want to break my three-year sobriety!"

I said, "Why, Mama?"

"Because you went to Mexico, I'm going to drink again! I'm going to and it's all your fault!"

I got off the phone with Mom and decided not to call her again for a while. I would let her cool off. I knew it wasn't my fault that she decided to drink again. I felt as if the devil spoke right through my mother to me. She did attempt to drink. But she had said that when she tried, something stopped her from swallowing and she knew it was an intervention from God. That was a miracle. I could tell my mom was beginning to put her trust into God.

At this time, I was pregnant again with my fourth child. Esperanza harassed me and became even more critical. I honestly thought she hated me. And, the closer I got to Jesus, the more Louis and I grew apart. He spent a lot of time with his mom. Her hurtful comments drove me to tears.

My mom had enough of both Louis and Esperanza's verbal abuse towards me, so she moved in. She was concerned that I was pregnant and going through so much. This made Esperanza stay away more because she did not want to cross my mom. Esperanza put pressure on Louis to make my mom leave. He seemed torn between me and his mom. But, Louis liked having my mom there because she had organizational skills and kept our house looking immaculate. I was not an easy target anymore as long as my mom stood by my side. I was very grateful because the stress from my husband and Esperanza had made me fear losing my baby.

Chapter 12

Hebrews 11:6 (NLT)

"And it is impossible to please God without faith. Anyone who wants to come to him must believe that God exists and that he rewards those who sincerely seek him."

1 Timothy 6:10 (NIV)

"For the love of money is a root of all kinds of evil. Some people, eager for money, have wandered from the faith and pierced themselves with many griefs."

Faith was in my heart and I started to feel a holy boldness come over me. I took Gods word literally. Everything God said was mine; I believed him. I was learning to walk by

faith and not by sight. The Holy Spirit himself was guiding each and every one of my steps.

One day, as I looked at my kitchen wall, I saw only bills, bills, bills. Louis and I literally had five dollars to our name. Suddenly, boldness came over me and I said out loud, pointing at the bills, "Satan, you must repay seven times everything you've stolen from me! In the name of Jesus!"

Later that evening, I went to a postal services center to mail a letter. When I walked in, I saw a display with free contest forms to win cash prizes.

I grabbed a few of the forms and put them in my pocket. When I got home, I sat at my kitchen table and filled the contest forms out. I needed to run to the grocery store, and asked Mom to watch the kids.

When I came back, I saw that Mom had organized the kitchen, and I couldn't find the contest forms. I asked Mom, "Mama, where are the contest forms I had on the table?"

She said, "Oh, I may have thrown them away!"

I replied, "No, Mama! That's my blessing!"

I retrieved them back from the garbage can, and they had no stains on them.

I gathered the kids and my mom and we went back to the postal center to submit the contest forms.

Before I went in, my family joined in prayer and we laid our hands over the forms. I remember praying, "The wealth of the wicked is laid up for the righteous, and that's me Lord!" I went into the postal center with a heart filled with faith, and dropped my forms into the entry box. As I walked away, I believed that God would give me what I asked for.

Soon, Mom's settlement for her accident would come through. Dad still had a heroin addiction, and wanted to use Mom and her money for his own gain. He put the pressure on her to move to a city where he could easily access his drugs. She began to listen to his advice and I prayed fervently about this.

Nothing I said to Mom seemed to deter her decision to take Dad's advice. I found my dad's character manipulative, controlling and convincing. Always a loyal wife, my mother wanted to believe him, I knew. But, I also knew the devil wanted to steal her money, and find a way to use it for something bad.

When she went to pick up her check, I told her, "Mother, Satan wants to rob you of all your money. He wants it to be wasted. You're listening to the wrong voice." Through the night, I interceded for my mom and her situation.

One evening, Louis and I talked as we headed for bed and he asked, "Lisa, when will we get our breakthrough [in our finances]?" I said to him, "God gave me two scriptures: to seek first His kingdom and His righteousness and everything else will follow (Matthew 6:33), and to build your business before your home (Proverbs 24:27). I don't know how God's going to do this, but I know he will."

The next morning, I got up early, made my husband's coffee, and kissed him goodbye. Then I fell back to sleep on the couch. Soon after, I got a phone call, but just missed it. The phone rang a second time, and I picked up and said, "Hello?"

A woman with a familiar voice asked, "Is this Lisa Moreno from California?"

I said, "Yes, it is."

She went on to ask if I remembered filling out a radio station's contest forms during Christmastime at the postal center. I said that I did, and she responded, "Well, Miss Lisa Moreno from California, you are the grand prize winner of ONE HUNDRED THOUSAND DOLLARS!" I screamed, feeling ecstatic. God had answered my prayer!

The call was broadcasted through the radio station from which I had won the contest—a station that many of my friends and family listened to. Celebratory messages filled my answer machine. Relatives and old friends asked, "Lisa, did your God do this?" "Lisa, is it because you tithe?"

I had left Louis a message on his work phone telling him what happened, and he called me back saying, "Babe! Really? I can't believe it! You knew! You said God would do it! God really spoke to you." He came home, and we rejoiced together.

Louis had good intentions and said, "Let's do what God wants us to do [with the money]." We talked about business ideas to make our money grow. For a few weeks he stayed clean. I told him that we should pray and wait on God for his wisdom. Louis, receptive, agreed. He praised the Lord for giving us a miracle, and all was well for a time.

I continued to pray earnestly for my mother. A day or two after I won the money, the police pulled Dad over and caught him with another woman and some drugs. He went to jail, and it woke my mom up to the truth. This time, she seemed ready to listen and knew what I had said held probity. Mom readied herself for a life change. She brought her drugs wrapped in a box with the inscription, 'I WANT JESUS MORE THAN THIS' to Carol's house. She gave the box to Carol and Matthew, much to their amazement.

Mom wanted Jesus with all her heart. What a great salvation!

Carol and Matthew called the police department to come and pick up the drugs.

Mom knew that God had intervened on her behalf. Her heart began to transform. She decided to come to Bible study and surrender all she had held onto. God took away both her desire to smoke weed and to drink alcohol.

The Bible was the first book Mom had ever read; she would sit and read it for hours. She listened to worship frequently, and let God's presence consume her. She loved Jesus, and he became her focus.

In the weeks following my contest win, I saw a depth of darkness that overtook Louis' eyes. He seemed like a different person and not in a good way. He spent his time in the company of Esperanza and his brother, Joe. One day, out of nowhere, Louis said, "You are going to give me half of that money when it gets here." I said, "What are you talking about Louis?" He said, "I want half of that money. I'm going to buy a motorcycle and a sports car. I deserve it, and legally, it's half mine."

"Louis, what happened to you? You said God did this and blessed us with the money. You said we would invest and make it grow!"

"If you don't Lisa, I will divorce you!" I told Louis, "Then you don't love me. I don't love the money, Louis. I don't care that much about it, but I refuse to give it to you for such evil things. You've been listening to the advice of your mother and brother; advice from the devil."

His comments devastated me, and I felt the strain even worse in my pregnant condition.

That same day, Joe called on the phone and when I answered, he cussed me out—loud enough to where Louis could hear. Louis said nothing. The phone call added another layer to the increase of turmoil in my life.

For some reason, my check took a while to arrive. Many times, Louis came home angry asking if the check came. I gave him the same answer again and again "No, Louis."

One day he said to me, "What's the hold up?!" I responded, "It's you; God isn't letting it be released yet because of you. I don't love the money Louis. It won't change me, but it has already changed you!"

Still, every day he asked about that check.

Satan caused great division in my marriage. Louis was never the same after his decision to give me an ultimatum, and although I still lived in our house, I rarely saw him because he went to his mom's house most of the time.

My life continued this way, and there was strain in our relationship. People took sides. Even some in my own family [who had not surrendered to God], took Louis's side.

Things seemed bizarre, and I grieved, but at the same time, I had to press more and more into Christ—the only stability in my life.

I could feel the Holy Spirit strengthening me to go on. I depended on his leading, and absolutely would not bow to the demands and threats of the devil—even if I lost everything.

I believed Louis thought I would just do what he said. But at this point, when I knew he'd been advised to divorce me, I drew a line in the sand. I chose God.

Even though hardship filled this period in my life, I saw God intervene many times. It reminded me of Moses and the Israelites when they tried to leave Egypt. God had hardened Pharaoh's heart, and things seemed hopeless. They felt pressure on every side, but God stayed right by them. He saw everything, and planned it all from beginning to end. He was their great defender.

I finally received a call to pick up my check in a week. Mom and I talked about what was the wisest way to handle our money. We really prayed and pondered it.

While we discussed her purchasing a house, I referenced the scripture Habakkuk 2:2, which talks about writing your vision and making it plain. So, on paper she wrote out specific things that she wanted in her house. I saw a picture in my head and drew her future home's door in detail.

For certain legal reasons, my mom planned to put the house in my name.

One day, after Louis finished arguing with me again about the money, he went into the living room. Mom and I had just started to pray in the kitchen, when all of the sudden, what sounded like a humongous hand smacked the wall and made our house shake.

It was amazing!

Mom and I both instinctively felt God's presence, and she loudly said, "I'm not putting the house in your name. I'm putting it in mine; I'll take my chances!"

Suddenly, Louis came running out of the living room screaming, "NO! You can't do that!"

It was the most bizarre thing. It seemed as if he'd planned something evil and his plan was foiled. God protecting us felt awesome. The proof my mom and I needed to know that we'd taken the right road with this decision. God had intervened.

In two days I would pick up my check. Louis called again to ask when the check would arrive, and I told him the truth. He said, "I'm going with you, and you better not go without me! Do you hear me?"

I prayed, not knowing what to do, but expecting God to step in again.

The next day, Louis behaved terribly to me. Then, after he left, I got a phone call from him. He was in the hospital, and when I asked what happened, he screamed, "Your God put me here!"

The hospital would not release him because he had mono and a liver infection. I called my mentor, Carol, and another friend and we went to see Louis at the hospital. I tried again to reason with him. Louis looked angry and once again threatened, "If you really loved me, you would give me the money! If not, I'll divorce you."

He looked very upset—even teary eyed. His selfishness had over-taken him. We ended up leaving because Louis responded unreasonably. I thought to myself, "He has sold his soul to the devil."

I could do nothing. No amount of reasoning with Louis would change his mind. It felt as if our marriage's division had come from Hell itself.

I went without Louis to pick up the check, and had fear in doing so, since he had warned me of the repercussions. I immediately deposited the check into a bank, and took out a portion out for my tithe. I wanted to get away to pray and stay out of Louis' wrath, so I stayed the night at a hotel along with Mom and my kids. It seemed ironic that about two hours after I banked the money, they released Louis from the hospital.

That night, I got a call from my Aunt Liz saying that Louis promised that if I came home, then he would be reasonable. **I'm still dumbfounded as to why she and certain other people in my** family comforted Louis at that time. It was very strange, especially since they were MY family!

So my naïve-self agreed to come home, and man, did I make a big mistake. Louis got in my mom's face as to intimidate her, screaming and cussing. I went to call the police, and as I talked on the phone, he ripped it out of the wall and out of my hand. My hand got cut. When the police arrived, they asked if we had any guns in the house, and I said, "Yes."

Later on, Louis told me that a few days prior, he heard a voice say to him, "Move the gun to your mom's house." So, no gun was found.

While outside, my mother-in-law bad-mouthed my mom and I to the police, starting more trouble. After staying fairly quiet about her behavior for all these years, I finally defended myself. Her mouth dropped when I asked the police to make her leave. She left, and Louis went with her.

I stayed in our home about two weeks with our children. I cried every day while living there. In my distress, I looked to God and my kids to give me peace.

At this time, Mom busily house hunted and had already looked at over thirty homes. She wanted to make a final decision, and aske if I would see the last one with her. I agreed to go.

God is so faithful; he heard our prayers that ver up to the house and said, "Mama, do you remember looked like on the picture of the house that I drew? That's the same door, and exactly the same glass pane!"

We walked into the house and stared at a picture of Jesus on the living room wall.

I said to Mom, "This is it! It's the house, Mama!"

Mom agreed, and she made the winning offer on the house.

A couple of weeks later, it came time for us to move. I would stay with my mom until I could figure out what was to happen with Louis and me.

Joe came over right before we left. He rode up on his motorcycle, walked into my house, came up to me and said, "You're really moving, huh? You didn't have to go; you could've stayed here." He stood up to my mom as if to intimidate her, and then left angry.

When I left that house, I felt [in the spirit] a huge release. If I had stayed there, it would have added another thing for Louis' family attempt to control me with.

I made a phone call to my father-in-law, Fernando who lived in another state. I told him everything that happened and explained that Esperanza meddled in our business and she wouldn't let her son grow up. I let him know about Louis's serious drug addiction. He believed I spoke the truth, and I hoped that he could talk and reason with Louis.

But Louis still didn't change. He called and yelled at me for telling his dad, but I did not regret having called, because his dad needed to know.

So, I moved into Mom's house, and felt very happy for her. Her house had a fenced-in swimming pool, just like she prayed for, and every other detail that she'd asked God for. She protected me greatly, and got her second chance to be the mom I needed. I still wanted to have my family whole, but had no idea how God planned to turn things around.

Chapter 13

Psalm 57:6 (NLT)

"My enemies have set a trap for me. I am weary from distress. They have dug a deep pit in my path, but they themselves have fallen into it."

A couple of days later, I went into labor. All that moving and stress probably made my son come a little early. I had someone call Louis to relay the message. Every other time I had a baby, Louis had stayed by my side. He'd cry when our kids were born, engaged and attentive to them. He cut every one of their umbilical cords. I never felt Louis looked at me with any disgust during labor. As a matter of fact, he'd tell me repeatedly that he thought I was beautiful. He was attracted to me, pregnant or not.

But this time, it was different. When he walked in, my heart hoped he'd changed. But he hadn't. Louis looked repulsed at my labor and the birth of our son. It hurt me badly to see him respond in that way.

I named our son Levi which means "joined in harmony." Louis wanted to name him something else, but I felt as though God made his name stand out when I searched for baby names.

While in the labor room, Louis went into my purse without me seeing and he stole a check to find out my banking information.

After Levi's birth, Louis practically begged me to let Esperanza come and see him, and I reluctantly agreed.

Before she came in, Carol, Matthew, and a deliverance minister came into the room and anointed Levi. They prayed over him, and the deliverance minister said, "Oh little Levi, you will be used for the Jews." It reminded me of the three wise men coming to bless Jesus. **Of course, he's not Jesus, but I mean the significance of an infant's birth and then receiving a blessing before any wicked thing could happen.** And blessed Levi was from the time of his birth.

Later, when Esperanza came in to see Levi, her only remark was: "You can tell he's going to have buck teeth."

I went home to my mom's the next day.

Two days after that, Joe came in through my mom's garage door and said, "Nice house," handed me divorce papers and continued, "You've been served!" When he left, I sobbed, and sobbed, and sobbed. I had prayed and prayed for Louis' heart to change. I had an empty feeling and a broken heart.

Not only had Louis filed for divorce, but he was also trying to get shared custody of the kids. He even had Mom's and my bank accounts seized since I was her beneficiary. The court papers also read something like, "I and the community are in danger of Ms. Moreno taking the money and giving it all away to the church and not paying her taxes."

This was so far from the truth! I had no money, no husband, and four small children to take care of. My world seemed to be falling apart.

Dad stayed friendly with my husband's family. Esperanza had said to him, "Oh Manuel, please tell your daughter do not get an attorney. We have one and he'll take care of everything."

I told my dad, "I'm not going to do that!"

Mom found an attorney for me named Paige, a woman whose house Mom used to clean. Paige had a reputation for being a "shark" in the courtroom; someone who didn't play around. She felt fondly toward Mom—a plus. We gave her a retainer for her services, and Paige got right on the job.

In the meantime, I had started attending a new church. I'd met a minister during my pregnancy. He worked as missionary, and prayed for people in the church. I had many uplifting conversations with him at church, and thought of him as only a friend.

But as soon as I had Levi, he came to my parents' house. He made me very uncomfortable as I was still a married woman, and still in love with Louis. He tried to compliment me in front of my dad, and it felt very awkward.

While alone in the kitchen, mom told me that maybe God wanted me with him. My mom, still young in Lord, hadn't too much of the word inside of her yet.

I replied, "I don't like him, Mom. And if he really worked for God, then he'd know it's not right to pursue a woman who still married."

The minister stayed there for hours trying to look at the deep things of my heart and said some things that I knew did not come from God, while other things he said were true, but obvious.

He tried to take us all out to dinner that night, and I respectfully declined and he left soon after.

He also tried many times to call me on the house phone, but I asked my parents not to pick it up. I would not speak to him again; I felt it was the first test after my separation from Louis.

It really came down to this: Would I trust in my heart what God had showed me about Louis, or would I try to go about things in my own way? I decided to trust God.

Loneliness is a very powerful emotion. This emotion can cause you to do funny things if not controlled. Throughout all the time I wasn't with Louis I had testing because I was lonely. I lived with a commitment in my heart to Louis and God. Even if Louis wasn't being honorable. I was going to be.

How can you date someone who is married or committed?

Just because you're lonely is that a good enough reason to let a committed person continue to flirt with you and never stop them.

You can't possibly be that desperate for attention. Hey if a married man is hitting on you, don't feel special. There is nothing special about that. Want excitement? Go skydiving. Want a thrill? Swim with a shark that should do the trick.

You may be married but lonely in your marriage. A word of advice: take the time to get close to God. The Bible says God is close to the brokenhearted. God will honor you for honoring him. Make the right decisions even if you're the only one around who is. Keep doing good. Pray before you make any life changing decisions. Please don't find comfort for your unhappy marriage in someone you're already attracted to. You may end up making a mistake and suffer the consequences for it.

If you have made mistakes get your heart right with God. Repent and really mean it. Believing for my marriage took great discipline and commitment. It also took a strength that I drew from God. It was not easy.

Chapter 14

Hebrews 11:1 (NLT)

"Faith is the confidence that what we hope for will actually happen; it gives us assurance about things we cannot see."

couple of weeks later, it came time for my first day at court. I had prayed throughout each day before I went, and God asked me, "Do you remember the Latin attorney [who tried to seduce me with his eyes a couple years before during Louis' trial]?" I said, "Yes, Lord." He said, "He will be there today." I replied, "I'm ready Lord."

Sure enough, as I waited in the courthouse with my new baby, the handsome Latin attorney walked up to me and tried to make small talk. He complimented me about my new baby and told me about himself. When we finished talking, I went into court.

Louis and his attorney made their plea, and the judge ordered us to go to mediation.

As I walked out of the courtroom, Mom handed me a business card, and said, "Lisa, that attorney (the one who had approached me earlier) talked to me when you were in court. He asked for you to call him. He said he's very attracted to you, and your husband's crazy."

I replied, "That's the devil, Mama."

She looked confused and questioned, "The devil?"

I said, "It reminds me of the fruit that Adam and Eve ate — looks good, smells good, tastes good, but it leads to death."

We left the courthouse and returned home.

A few Christian advisors had told me to keep the card; that I might need that attorney's legal advice. I kept the card for a week, but it burned a hole in my pocket. I didn't plan to call him, so I ended up throwing his card away. Louis and I had separated only a month before, and I had already been tested twice. God had given me the desire to reunite with my husband, and I would not make room for doubt.

The real testing, though, came from some of my "Christian" friends. I heard them say some of the most doubtful and hopeless statements. I apparently frustrated some people with my faith talk. I think they spent more time trying to convince me of all the reasons why "it was impossible," rather than building me up my faith. My friends said things like, "Too much has gone wrong," or, "He'll never change."

But I believe God saved me first for a reason. It is mind-boggling to me that I gave my heart to Jesus not even two months after being married to Louis. I always believed it was God's will for me to make sure he received salvation. Already I had seen so many people come to Jesus who seemed hopeless, and I knew that truly nothing was impossible for God.

I tried to have happiness with my new baby and my little children, but it was difficult to control my stress. The court had ruled that my children would spend every other weekend with Louis at Esperanza's house, and it worried me greatly. The only child Louis never took with him was Levi—it was almost like he had a fear of taking him. God must have been protecting my son from danger.

Although I wasn't going to change my mind, the unbelief that my marriage would be restored by friends and family was grieving my spirit. I know most people meant well and wanted to protect me, but I had already made a decision. Mom believed with me—she was full of faith.

My friend Mary also believed with me, and posed the question, "What do you want?" When I told her I wanted to believe for my marriage, she replied simply, "Then believe."

One night I made a decision to fast and pray. Only God knew I was fasting and praying, and I was trusting that He would hear my prayers. I said to God, "I don't care what anybody says, if you tell me to believe for him, I will believe you, Lord!"

So on the third day, I woke up and heard father God speak to me: "I Am. I Am putting my heart into him. I Am. I Am making him a praying husband. I Am. I Am making him a praying father. I Am. I Am doing a new thing. I Am." I then said to God, "I can go on Lord!"

"If you have never heard the audible voice of God, it more amazing than anything I can put into words. If you have, you know what I mean.

Chapter 15

Psalm 23:5 (NLT) "You prepare a feast for me in the presence of my enemies. You honor me by anointing my head with oil. My cup overflows with blessings."

Isaiah 61:3 (NLT) "He will give a crown of beauty for ashes, a joyous blessing instead of mourning, festive praise instead of despair. In their righteousness, they will be like great oaks that the LORD has planted for his own glory."

One day, my children came home from being with their dad. Lani looked like she had tears in her eyes, and I asked her what was wrong. She told me that her father had a girlfriend, and she had met her. I felt crushed. Although Louis and I were separated, it still came as a bitter shock to me. I believed for our marriage and family, and we just had a son. And, I still greatly loved him.

I waited for my family to leave the house so I could be alone.

I threw myself on the ground in great anguish, screaming, "God, I can't take anymore! Please, I can't take this!" My pain was so great.

That evening, it was with a heavy heart that I went to Bible study. I didn't mention to anyone what had happened with Louis. There was an empty chair in the middle of the room and for whoever needed prayer.

I told God stubbornly, "I'm not going to sit in that chair, Lord."

I heard a small, inner voice say, "Sit in the chair."

I responded, "Yes, Lord."

Reluctantly, I sat in the chair. An elder from my church came up and started to pray over me. He said, "There are [spiritual] chains that are binding you. Your friends are going to pray for you and break those chains."

My friends came to me and prayed that God would heal my broken heart and help me get through everything I was facing.

Then, the most amazing thing happened. As my eyes were closed and hands lifted, I felt an overwhelming sense of peace. In that peace, I then felt a pouring of warm anointing oil on my head. The rich, spicy smell of the frankincense and myrrh was so intoxicating. It was just heavenly. The oil kept pouring and pouring—they must have poured a whole quart of oil on my head already!

The more oil that poured, the more peace I felt. I could hear the pitter-patter of the oil dripping from my head onto my lap. Oh, it was astonishing. It was as God was giving me a personal touch from heaven.

When the praying was over, I opened my eyes and asked, "Who put all that oil on my head?"

Everyone in the room responded, "Nobody!"

I feel my hair, face, and clothes, and I am completely dry. I realized it was God himself anointing me, and I was completely in awe.

I left Carol's house renewed and the anguish and despair that I'd felt was completely gone. I continued to intercede for Louis, and "called those things are not as if they were" *(Romans 4:17)*.

Soon after, at another court date, Louis showed up with his new attorney, Mr. Herrington. In Louis' declaration, he stated that he would like to sue the church that I gave a tithe to.

I told my attorney, Paige, "I don't care about my money just don't let them touch my tithe because that's my blessing."

Mr. Herrington made Louis' plea on this matter, and when it was stated, the judge quickly stood from his chair in anger and declared, "No one's going to sue a church in my courtroom!"

Paige and I were shocked, eyes widened, while Mr. Herrington and Louis looked frightened. Mr. Herrington was stumbling on his words, apologized to the judge for even bringing it up, and the judge told him he was to drop the subject, and to forget about whatever money was given to the church.

Later was our court-ordered mediation with Louis and me. The mediator looked so stressed out. I kept thinking to myself, "This man is in the wrong business."

I don't think he was necessarily taking Louis's side but he wasn't taking my side either. He seemed irritated that Louis and I were even there, and it seemed to pain him when we had something to say. I offered to pay for Louis to take a hair follicle test in order to prove that he was on drugs, and requested to keep our kids in my care until Louis finished a drug program. Legally, he could not be forced to take one, and strongly opposed to it. The mediator looked puzzled, but let it go.

Chapter 16

Proverbs 27:10 (NIV)

"Do not forsake your friend or a friend of your family, and do not go to your relative's house when disaster strikes you—better a neighbor nearby than a relative far away."

Matthew 19:13–15 (MSG)

"One day children were brought to Jesus in the hope that he would lay hands on them and pray over them. The disciples shooed them off. But Jesus intervened: "Let the children alone, don't prevent them from coming to me. God's kingdom is made up of people like these." After laying hands on them, he left."

*O*ne day, my friend Mary stopped talking to me out of the blue. My prayer warrior friend who I loved like a sister cut our friendship off. I called her phone over and over again, and she never returned my call. We still attended the same weekly Bible study and had small talk, but I didn't mention anything serious because she seemed uninterested—I felt like Mary had rejected and abandoned me.

Carol saw me cry for weeks because of my ended friendship with Mary. I had already lost so much, and now I had lost my best friend. Although I was hurt, I had accepted the fact that our friendship was over. She would be there for me and helpful during an urgent crisis, but then disappeared as soon as the worst was over.

Mary's husband, Jonathan, was a leader at the Bible study we all attended. After a while, he started to treat my children cruelly— as though my children and I weren't good enough to be around him and his family.

A time when this was expressed was a night at Bible study when he said to my son Louis Jr. in front of other children, "Go change your diaper—you stink."

He laughed to mock Louis Jr., and the children around him joined in. My son ran into the bathroom crying. I ran after Louis in the bathroom since I had seen what had just happened from across the room. Jonathan had humiliated my son. When I saw my son cry and he explained what had happened, I was angry. Jonathan knew all that my children had went through recently, and his actions were uncalled for—especially coming from a Christian leader.

I walked up to Jonathan and said, "What you said to my son was not nice, if he stinks like you say, it is because he has had encopresis (a problem with the bowel) since he was a baby. You embarrassed him. It's not funny to him, he's in the bathroom crying."

Jonathan responded, "Oh I didn't know."

That was all he said—this couple who I'd admired and trusted had turned their back on me and my kids. My children's feelings were hurt at this treatment, and they told me so. I taught my children to pray for them and to not hate them.

Over the years, I have come to realize that it can be easy for people who are put in church leadership to forget where they came from if they are not careful. Forming elite groups or cliques in the church is a worldly way of being. Jesus dealt with the "Elite Groups." They were supposed to love God and do his will. But instead they became puffed up with pride, loving the praise of the people instead of running after God. They were looked up to, the ones who were to teach the people God's ways. Jesus said they didn't practice what they preached. They were jealous of Jesus, the anointed one. All heaven backed him up and he did the will of the father. He went around doing good, loved on the people. He was willing to go where the priests refused to go. He was willing to talk to those the priests weren't willing to talk to. They were spiritual snobs and only cared about themselves. Jesus

was and still is the real deal. He is our example. So if you have been hurt by the elite ones, just know Jesus doesn't care for that behavior. He would meet with you talk with you and love you. No matter what you have done in the past, Jesus can help you. He loves you so much.

Chapter 17

Joel 2:28 (KJV)

*"And it shall come to pass afterward, that I will pour
out my spirit upon all flesh; and your sons and your
daughters shall prophesy, your old men shall dream
dreams, your young men shall see visions."*

During this time, I had a dream. In the dream, I was in a
department store and saw the woman who I had a physical
altercation with many years before. I saw her in the store, and heard
the voice of Jesus say, "Will you even tell her my gospel, Lisa?"

I responded, "Yes, Lord!"

The next day I was in that very store that I'd dreamt about, and
there she was: the very woman who I had seen in the dream.

I walked up to her and said, "Hi Samantha, I know this is going
to sound crazy, but I had a dream about you."

I explained to her my dream, and then apologized for anything I'd done to hurt her. I told her I was now a Christian, and a changed person.

She put her head down and said, "You don't know all I've done."

I understood, and shared that God could wash it all away. Right there in the store, she allowed me to pray for her. I felt sincere love and compassion for her well-being, and for her soul. It was divine intervention that I would run into her there, just as in my dream.

I had signed up to go on a second missionary trip to Mexico. I was short on money to go, and did not know how I would afford food on the trip.

A friend asked, "Are you sure God told you to go?"

I kept praying about it. I was getting ready to leave the house the day before the trip when my mom asked where I was headed. I responded, "I'm going to Wal-Mart, Mama! God told me He's going to give me a miracle."

I was walking around Wal-Mart with Levi (my other kids were with their Dad) when a Wal-Mart employee came up to me, looked at Levi and said, "Your baby—he holds the presence of God! I'm off work now. Can you wait here while I grab my things? I have something for you."

I agreed to, and when she came back and told me to hold out my hands.

She placed a hundred dollar bill in my hands and said, "God says you know what this is for. He says that He's seen your fiery trials and is very proud of you. God says not to listen to the voices around you, for you do hear [his] voice. He knows you're worried about the deliverance of your husband, but he says you have a double portion of deliverance in your hands."

She started speaking about Levi, and said he would draw many children to the Lord. She prayed for protection for us and I left Walmart so happy.

My mom was going on the missionary field with me for the first time. She was such a miracle. She was truly happy just to be belong to God. So my mom brought a lot of money with her on the trip and she was blessing the people of Mexico. She had faith and joy in the Lord. Mom reminded me of Zacchaeus in the Bible, he was so grateful to Jesus, that he wanted to give his things away.

My mom sat in the backseat with our friend Dottie the whole time on the way to Mexico. Dottie was the sweetest Christian lady. She had so much patience with my mom. Dottie answered a lot of her questions.

Another thing my mom did was have a well built in an African village. She was so happy to be a good to those less fortunate than her.

When we came back I was pretty broke, but I was praying for God's help to meet my needs. When I looked in the mailbox there was an envelope waiting for me. The name was unfamiliar. The check was for $150.

Later I remembered who this person was. I had prayed for a man's salvation before I left on my trip. He had been an atheist, and said my talk with him really impacted his life. Praise the Lord! I really didn't know how much it meant to him, but I was so glad to hear it.

Chapter 18

1 Samuel 16:7 (NLT)

But the LORD said to Samuel, "Don't judge by his appearance or height, for I have rejected him. The LORD doesn't see things the way you see them. People judge by outward appearance, but the LORD looks at the heart."

*L*evi, my little baby was about to be one year old. I planned a big birthday party for him. We got a jumper and I had arts and crafts for the children to do. When Louis showed up to the party he had a hickey on his neck. This probably shouldn't have surprised me, but it did.

Seeing this really threw me for a loop and crushed me. I loved him so much. There was a sick feeling in my stomach. The betrayal, and now, the adultery, felt like a knife cutting into my heart. There wasn't anything I could do to make him see that what he did was wrong.

While at a Bible study, Carol made comments about my clothing, how I should change the way I dressed. It hurt my feelings especially when it was in front of other people, including my kids. I had friends witness this and ask me if I felt bad when Carol would say these things to me. I would brush it off and say she was only trying to help. She would do some kind things for me, like buy me clothes without me being there. Nice things but not my taste. So I really didn't know how to take it, except that maybe my appearance, in her eyes, needed to change, and was not good enough.

I dealt with accepting Carol for who she was, and tried to overlook her mistreatment of me. Although I could have defended myself more, I wanted show Carol respect. I think deep inside of me, I was hungry for parental approval. I wanted someone to say "You're doing a good job. I'm proud of you." Something was missing inside of my heart and at times, Carol provided the validation I was searching for. At other times, she was like a strict, angry parent.

I've learned something, not everything a Christian says is necessarily "thus sayeth the Lord, "a word from God, or what's best for you. Sometimes when giving advice people are in their flesh and not hearing it directly from God. God has given us discernment to know the difference.

What I did feel was a lot of condemnation and that I wasn't measuring up to her standards. Then there were times that there was love between us and she could be an understanding, older friend. I was compared to her daughter, my children to her grandkids, and I to other Christian women. I homeschooled, that was an issue for Carol, she told me often. My kids would hear some of these conversations, and I regret not putting a stop to many things. **But I forgive myself and since then, I have asked my kids for their forgiveness for keeping them in that negative environment.**

I didn't realize until years later what a terrible thing it was for me to allow Carol to put me down the way I was. This happened while my daughter was standing there. She was too small to speak up then. But when my daughter got older, she told me how it pained her to hear me being put down by Carol in the years we were at Bible study.

I should have realized the negative way it would affect my daughter. But I didn't. I was blind to it. I thought I was being respectful by taking it. I was wrong.

God didn't make me to fit into a mold, made by people.

I have a testimony that God gave me so I can help another.

The way you look, the family you are born into, the lessons you've learned in life, even your past sins, our mistakes and triumphs God uses it all for the Greater Good.

I've realized that I'm approachable to certain people, we all are.

My life experiences may make the person I'm speaking to feel understood, and that's important. The laidback way I dress sometimes, in jeans and t-shirts, is not appalling to God. God does not judge by outward appearance. God looks in a person's heart.

My life experiences have made me into the person I am today. And God has a purpose for my life. He has a plan for your life too!

Chapter 19

Luke 14:15–24 (NLT)

"Hearing this, a man sitting at the table with Jesus exclaimed, "What a blessing it will be to attend a banquet in the Kingdom of God!"

Jesus replied with this story: "A man prepared a great feast and sent out many invitations. When the banquet was ready, he sent his servant to tell the guests, 'Come, the banquet is ready.' But they all began making excuses. One said, 'I have just bought a field and must inspect it. Please excuse me.' Another said, 'I have just bought five pairs of oxen, and I want to try them out. Please excuse me.' Another said, 'I now have a wife, so I can't come.'

"The servant returned and told his master what they had said. His master was furious and said, 'Go quickly into the streets and alleys of the town and

*invite the poor, the crippled, the blind, and the lame.'
After the servant had done this, he reported, 'There is
still room for more.' So his master said, 'Go out into
the country lanes and behind the hedges and urge
anyone you find to come, so that the house will be
full. For none of those I first invited will get even the
smallest taste of my banquet.'"*

1 Corinthians 9:22–23 (NIV)

*"To the weak I became weak, to win the weak. I have
become all things to all people so that by all possible
means I might save some. I do all this for the sake of
the gospel that I may share in its blessings."*

*M*y mom and I were coming into membership at church this day. My daughter Lani was getting baptized the same day. Lani's dad Louis was invited to the church. I didn't know if he would come or not.

I had been visiting this church for many years and I always wanted to make it my home church.

I also told my dad Manuel to come. He had recently been diagnosed with a Brain Tumor. I had not told the Pastors anything about his situation. My dad and I weren't talking much to each other at this time. He was living a crazy life of drugs and still on the streets.

This is what my dad said about this day he came to church. "I heard the most beautiful voice singing. Her voice drew me to the front of the church."

This was a big church and my dad didn't see me and my mom. All of a sudden the Pastor walked up to my dad and begins to give him a prophetic word publicly. He said to my dad, "God wants to speak a word into you, it's a word of encouragement and a word of warning. The word of warning is after the lord touches you, you can't return back to the place you've been. You cannot follow the crowd that you have followed, you cannot associate with the people you've associated with."

The pastor continued, "I'm not saying they are all bad people, they are probably very nice people in the natural and could be good friends in some ways. But let me just tell you they're tearing you down they are tearing you apart. I've never seen you and I don't know you, but telling you right now never again never again, your life's over, you've got to be free!"

"You've got to be free, Hallelujah to walk in the ways of God!"

"We're speaking liberation in Jesus name. "Then my dad whispered something in the Pastors ear.

The Pastor said, "He says his wife and daughter are here. Come, where are you?

My mother and I came to the front of the church.

The Pastor said, "They got baptized today and came into membership. He looked at my mom and said" you've been delivered of an addiction too."

My mom replied, "Thirty years."

"Hallelujah she was baptized, everyone stretch out your hands."

My parents and I were in the front of the church at this time. The Pastor than said "Lord unite this family, Satan has come to try and tear up this relationship and to tear up this family, but he is not going to succeed because the lord is doing a miracle right now amen. The lord has called you into freedom and liberty, from this time he's going to take you into a new dimension. It's a new beginning for your family, it's a starting all over. It's a washing away of the past and it's a new door. It's a new time place an open door into the presence of the lord will break it!"

He looked at my mom and said "Daughter, you've walked in fear. There have been attacks against your mind, against your body, and against your spirit. You've wondered at times how long can I continue. How can I go on with the pressures there's been. You've looked for stability and it hasn't always been there. But the lord says, I've come to bring a fresh joy into you, daughter—a fresh peace. Fresh healing, emotional healing for this heavy depression that comes upon you at times and just wants to suck you up and eat and swallow you. It's like a cloud—you don't even know when it's coming. It just swoops you up, you feel suicidal at times and the lord says I lift that from off of you. It evaporates now and healing is coming to your spirit, and to your mind and heart. Freedom!

Then he looked at me and said, "And daughter there's a call on you! There's a word of God in your mouth. There's an evangelistic anointing upon you, wherever you go you're going to speak the word of the lord. You're going to be like a magnet and people are going to be drawn to you, they're going to feel a sense of the spirit of God upon you. People are going to get saved in the streets, they're going to call on the name of the lord, they are going to get down and bow before their maker! Because of the hand of the lord! The word of the lord will not return Void!"

The Pastor continued speaking over us, "It's been said about this family, even people have looked upon them, people that know them, people close to them, relatives have said, I don't think they are going to make it. They are most unlikely to succeed because of the demonic spirits that have come against this household. Today we cancel out all of that in the name of The Lord. And we say there is a brand new chapter, a brand new day, a brand new future, because of the power of God resting upon them."

Looking at my mom, a prophetic woman said, "The Lord is showing me that you've been walking around with a robe of guilt on you. There's been a generational assignment against you from another generation. We break the power of witchcraft! We break it right now, you fowl spirit I command you to take your hands off these people, in the powerful wonderful and great name of Jesus.

The enemy has even said to you that you have to be like the generation before you. You're trapped you can't do anything else but the lord will announce in your ear this day that you're free. The blood of Jesus and break every Generational curse and there shall not be an accusation against you that shall prosper. All the voices that you have consulted or your family has consulted in the past shall not be charged against you says the Lord. The lord would say, there is a deliverance that has come to you and loose you from the grip you've been in. The robe is coming off of you and you shall declare a freedom says the Lord.

Then they all prayed for my family.

Chapter 20

Matthew 18:8–9 (MSG)

"If your hand or your foot gets in the way of God, chop it off and throw it away. You're better off maimed or lame and alive than the proud owners of two hands and two feet, godless in a furnace of eternal fire. And if your eye distracts you from God, pull it out and throw it away. You're better off one-eyed and alive than exercising your twenty-twenty vision from inside the fire of hell."

We had heard about a camp in the mountains, a retreat the church was having. I took my kids and my parents up to this retreat. When I explained to my parents that a Puerto Rican pastor would be there, it made the deal a little sweeter. My dad loves the fact that he is Puerto Rican.

When we went, my parents were giving me a hard time. They were just being difficult. I was determined to get my parents prayer from this minister. Boy did we ever get prayer.

In a meeting at camp after the Puerto Rican Pastor preached, he walked up to my dad and prayed about him being in the world still, that he compromised.

He then prayed for mom about the spirit of witchcraft that was against her and she was slain in the spirit. Laying out on the ground, she was touched by God.

Then the Pastor walked up to me and said, "Do you realize what has happened?" He said, "Your whole family is saved. Salvation and deliverance are in your hands."

He continued, "I know this may sound crazy, but you're going to lay hands on furniture and clothing and people will weep at the presence of God. He said, "God says I'm going to put back relationships that have been severed, even those that have been completely severed. I'm even putting those back together again."

Just then I saw their faces flash before my eyes as he prayed, my husband and my mother in law is who I saw. This word over me helped a lot by encouraging me as I keep believing for Louis. I was so encouraged.

Soon after, dad went back to his old ways and he then needed brain surgery. They gave us good and bad news. The doctors told us he had a 50/50 chance of survival and even if he survived they were unsure of what his condition would be. He got brain surgery they had to go through his skull to get to the brain.

We waited; my mom, myself, and many relatives. A lot of them were panicked that he wouldn't make it. My mom and I believed and stayed strong praying the whole time that he would recover. We knew God wasn't done with him yet. The surgeon cut through Pituitary gland, which made him 75% blind and the doctor wasn't sure if he would totally recover mentally. They weren't sure of what any of the outcome would be. Even though my parents were separated, my mom was willing to care for my dad and allow him to come to her new home. He really needed her. She forgave him for all he had done. She remembered how he was there for her when she had her car accident. When my dad came home he was so needy.

He acted as if he had Alzheimer's disease, he wasn't remembering much. He was physically and mentally challenged after surgery. He would have outbursts and insist on his medications when it wasn't time. He would wander around which could of danger to him because he wasn't all there. We could never leave him. One of us had to watch over him. He would jump up out of his sleep moaning. My mom was afraid he would drown in the pool. My mom started getting panicked about this difficult situation.

Within weeks he started becoming more alert and talking. He took a special interest in my baby Levi. Every morning he couldn't wait to see the baby. He would grab the baby and take him to the bathroom window sit him on the ledge and they would look at all the birds. He very slowly got better. I feel Levi helped my dad through this hard time of transition. He had to learn how to live with blindness. It was very hard on his manhood, because he was always so strong. It reminds me a little of Samson in the bible. How he was such a strong man but blinded.

I started to feel I wanted my own place. So I prayed every day. I had put my name on a list for low income subsidized apartments when I first left Louis.

It had been almost two years of waiting on this list and living with my parents. One morning I woke up and I felt led to go and get boxes and start packing. I love my parents but it was hard to live there at times. I packed in faith, I knew my time would be coming soon to move.

One day Louis Sr. showed up to my mom's door unexpected. I looked at him. He said, "Hi, Lisa"

I instinctively knew he needed me, though I saw no visible sign physically on him, I had a feeling he was in an accident. I said, "You've been in an accident." He said no. He had adoration in his eyes for me. I said, "Let me see your arms."

He let me see his arms, he was in pain and I knew it.

I said, "I'm calling the ambulance!"

He said, "No, Lisa, please don't call." I said, "OK, but you have to let me drive you there." He agreed.

I drove him there, he fractured his arm. While sitting there he told me, "Thank you, Lisa."

I knew he still loved me he had that look again, such adoration and gratitude that I cared.

Again a few weeks later Louis called me, "Lisa will you please let me take you guys to dinner." I said, "You want me to go?" He said Please Lisa will you come too?" I said, "alright Louis but you have to be nice." He said he would be.

I went with to the restaurant with our children. We sat at the table with him. Louis just sat there crying and holding our children. He wouldn't tell me why he was so upset.

He told me he loved me and he loved our children. I thought to myself, "Something is very wrong." Louis didn't say anything but kept repeating that he loved me and loved our kids very much. He continued to cry.

Years later I found out why. Louis without my knowing had started, with the money from my winnings and bought himself the motorcycle and sports car. He knew a lot of people and started bouncing at clubs. Eventually he brought in people, being a sociable guy and started getting bands gigs. He was getting big in business fast, promoting these bands. Some people who were bigger than him business wise, in these shifty clubs got jealous. They told Louis, "We know your wife and your children's names. We know where they live if you don't stop your business we will kill them." These people were dangerous. Louis at this time was dealing with some evil people.

He told me many years later. He said this really scared him. The thought of him losing his family, of us getting killed because of what he was doing, was more then he could bear.

Chapter 21

Matthew 21:22 (NLT)

"You can pray for anything, and if you have faith, you will receive it."

$\mathcal{M}$y name came up to move into the apartments I had been waiting for.

My income a week prior was cut drastically because Louis no longer had a job. He was working on the side I knew it, but I couldn't prove it. My faith would be challenged to move with very little income.

So I moved, walking by faith. My friends helped move my stuff. Once I moved into a sparsely furnished apartment with my four children I sat in the middle of my living room floor. I said to the Lord, "How are you going to take care of me?" I heard his still small inner voice say to me, "I'm going to use my body." I then saw a vision of a check that read Lisa Moreno $500. I said, "Oh thank you Lord!"

The next day I received a call from a friend I had not seen in almost three years. She had explained she couldn't get me out of her head, she kept thinking of me. She said she had something for me, but it wasn't much. The following day there she was my beautiful friend Lori with a check that said Lisa Moreno $500. I jumped, screamed, and hugged my friend. She cried, it blessed her just as much because she heard from God.

I had many more miracles during this time of my life. I will forever call this time of my life, "Gods provision in a time of famine." God takes care of his children. I know he was watching out for me like a husband and father to my children. We needed to feel safe and cared for.

Levi was a baby when a prophet was coming to our church. My friend Ray and I went. She helped me with my baby. I wasn't even at the front but the anointing was so strong in the church. She was prophesying over people randomly in the audience.

As I started walking down the aisle to go sit down she called out to me, she said, "Lady with the black sweatshirt!" I looked up and she said "You have such a heart for the deep things of God." She said "You are a prophetic evangelist; you'll have words for people." She said I was going to the streets, that I was a leader and I would take teams of women with me. She said that we would minister to young people on the street to front of bars.

She continued to speak to me saying, "You will go and speak Life, you will speak life. You have such heart for women have been raped, sexually abused and molested by the fathers and uncles."

And the whole time she's praying for me my body shaking under the anointing, I felt the presence of God so strong, consuming me. She told me I have been misunderstood that I have changed and I am changing and that I've been in a box and she cried out "we break the box open! We are kicking the box open, breaking the box breaking the box over your life."

She then addressed the fears that came against my life. "You have night terrors, we cancel the spirit of witchcraft, The witchcraft in your family from generations before." She prayed for me regarding this and I felt great!

Chapter 22

Ephesians 5:19 (NIV)

"Speaking to one another with psalms, hymns, and songs from the Spirit. Sing and make music from your heart to the Lord."

The Lord started encouraging through songs that seemed to speak to my current circumstances. My kids felt the same way. When Louis Sr. would hear these songs, he would mention how much he liked them. This really surprised me. It was such an encouraging thing to hear.

I started hearing music on the radio that made me feel so encouraged. In particular, the music of Jeremy Camp, a man who had lost his wife to cancer, built us up. He had a song called "Walk by Faith" and another called, "I'll Take you Back" which seemed to be about the prodigal son and "I Still Believe." All of his songs seemed to pertain to me, Louis and our kids. We were believing for this prodigal son to come home. The process was very difficult and often we would belt out his music to increase our faith. This kind of music helped us out so much.

I prayed for Louis every single day for many, many years. One day I felt an urgency to speak with him. I never called him unless it pertained to the kids. This time it was God moving on my heart to give him a call and invite him to Bible study. There was going to be a guest speaker, Pastor Dan.

I called Louis and said, "Louis I would like you to come to Bible study tonight. He said "no I don't want to go." He sounded so depressed to me, but again I felt inspired to say "please Louis come to Bible study." I feel like you're supposed to be there, the pastors going to be there too."

He came! Our children ran to him and gave him lots of love. I knew that meant a lot to him. Pastor Dan prayed for him and gave him a word from the Lord. We were all praying and he approached Louis he said, God was taking the sword from his back. He said he has made a lot of bad decisions, that he was influenced by the voices around him and that the voices were from the devil.

Louis cried and looked so much better. But, I didn't know the extent of troubles he had went through that night. Our family was being restored. My children and I were so happy to have Louis in our lives. We started seeing each other again and Louis bought me a new engagement ring.

He started going with us to church. He wrote out and shared his testimony with the pastors of our church. When we wrote Louis's testimony out, he said to me "Lisa there's a lot of things I did, are you ready to hear it?"

He said, "I hope you'll forgive me for what I did, I'm going to talk about the things, and I've been with other woman." I said, "It's okay, I already knew in my heart, I already forgave you."

This is his testimony.

Chapter 23

Romans 7:15 (NLT)

*"I don't really understand myself, for I want to do what
is right, but I don't do it. Instead, I do what I hate."*

Testimony by Louis Moreno written on February 8, 2006

Three Years Lost

"Me and my wife of almost 9 years are sitting outside the court finalizing our property and submitting our divorce papers. As soon as I sign those papers, it was like I made a deal with the devil. My life soon spiraled out of control with thoughts of bitterness, anger and betrayal. After we were given our money from our assets, it was a substantial amount of money, even after paying off bills and Money owed for lawyer fees. It consumes me so much to the point that I lavish myself with a sports car and a Harley Davidson which I thought I deserved for all the long and hard work I did in the past. So with these new idols keen people that entered my life for all the wrong reasons, because I had money and lavish myself with nice things.

Soon after I went looking for people that I thought were my friends, but were only there for the drugs and alcohol I could supply from my money that I had obtained. My addiction overtook me to the point of no return. At this time, I started going bar hopping trying to get back some kind of youth. I thought I missed out by being married with children at an early age. I started being promiscuous with an array of different women. This changed my outlook on life.

I changed from a loving introverted person to an angry and bitter person who fought anyone in my path. I was consuming alcohol, marijuana, and, occasionally, cocaine on the weekends. This led to "every other day" use and then using whenever I could get it. Soon, cocaine was not effective enough for me, so I started taking meth. It overtook my being and turned me into a person who I thought was invincible. It gave me energy, confidence, and a loss of appetite. I was changing my look from a man with a slight weight problem, to a person with sudden weight loss due to my fond addiction to meth.

Also I joined the gym and did very strenuous workouts. I lost a lot of weight and bulked up somewhat, which led me to others noticing the drastic change my appearance. My life was lonely, I had no remorse for my ex-wife or for my children. I started writing my motorcycle with my brother, which was really rewarding to me, because of the freedom I felt, while riding. I ran into a friend at the gym and we went to a club in a bar on the river, which I befriended the owner and which at this time I was surrounding myself with people in rock bands and DJs. He noticed that I knew a lot of people in the music business and asked me if I wanted to work for him as head of security and a bouncer and music promoter on the weekends. Since receiving this money I had not considered going back to my full-time job, which I was at for four years. I obtained a high level of its success, because of my bitterness towards my ex-wife and the child support, alimony, the courts had ordered me to pay. My addiction would not allow me to do so. So I obtained this job to obtain an income.

I started getting well-known in the bay area because of the turnaround I brought to this club. It became a hotspot because of my influence. Soon after I joined a notorious motorcycle Club. This boosted my ego and confidence to a different level. I felt this Club filled the void because of my loss of the relationship with my family. Soon after joining I brought in the owner of the club and a couple of other people as members. The president of the motorcycle club was starting to get jealous of me and my brother.

First off the president came after my brother and soon I followed. Before I was out of the motorcycle club we went to Reno for huge motorcycle rally. I had just customized my bike before heading to the rally. I went all day without sleeping from my usage of meth. While heading there I drank water with a liquid form of meth. This kept me up for the whole time I was in Reno.

One night I was staying with a member of the club on the outskirts of Reno. After being up for three days I went looking for his house and got lost and I veered around the corner at a high speed. I felt something glaring to the right of me trying to get my attention, a demon and it said "hey!" This distracted me. I turned my head and I lost control of my bike. I crashed and totaled my bike, which two days prior customized.

Some guy must have seen the crash, he came and picked up my mangled body from the ground. I returned home without being a member of the club due to the drama which affected me and my brother. I came back home and I started a deep dark battle with depression and self-pity. I did not have any kind of motivation or strength to obtain my well-being, the days came quickly upon me. While my financial needs were non-existing due To my isolation towards the world.

I found myself in a deep dark dungeon in which I pretty much slept and I had no ambition to continue. The heart of my depression was so big that I can get out of it. To the point where days turned into weeks and weeks turn into months and months turned into years. Due to my self-destruction from my drug abuse I've forgotten times, dates and responsibilities. During this time I had obtained a substantial amount of debt. I owed roughly $50,000 in child support, spousal and back taxes. I did not pay it because I used the money to lavish myself in a downward lifestyle.

I am here only by others prayers and forgiveness. I did not expect to be here as long as I am. Due to my unwillingness to obtain a living and prosperity to this point today I found myself going to see my children on February 6, 2006 and my wife asking me If I wanted to go to Carol's. I replied yes, but I knew I probably wouldn't go doing due to me being a procrastinator. I went home from my wife Lisa's. I went to my room and started weeping in my bed and many thoughts started flashing before me. I felt the presence of three or more demons pressing on my brain once name was self-pity, another named unworthiness, and still another the biggest one of all procrastination. They were throwing thoughts of suicide of me slicing my wrist with a razor blade. So I lifted myself from my bedroom and proceeded to take a shower while still having thoughts of suicide. I was weeping in the shower.

I composed myself and felt like God was calling me to go to Carol's. The only reason I went was because Lisa told me the pastor was going to be there. I was hoping he would have some encouraging words, since I was going to start a new job driving construction trucks. I haven't done this in a while, hoping I still remember how to drive one. I was hoping to stay with that Company to pursue some endorsement requirements for driving vehicles. I walked into Carol's and saw Lisa standing there and my children came up to me I was holding my children and this all comforted me. And after pastor spoke I was hoping he would notice me somewhat. Carol told Lisa to get me and have pastors pray over me. Usually I am standoffish and very unwilling to accept guidance. But after all I have gone through I decided to give it a shot, since my life up to this point has been unmanageable. His words were very inspiring to me in which I broke down and front of a mass amount of people. I never thought I would let someone come into my heart and feel my pain. I felt an uplifting in myself in the words of encouragement and it is my will to sustain my rebuilding of my life, my family and doing so I hope to obtain my forgiveness from my wife and children. I lost three and unbearable and very treacherous and demoralizing for years. Today I feel like a weight has been lifted off me. I am going to change my outlook on my future with a walk with Christ and with those who love me unconditionally. This is an awakening."

We had decided to leave out a part of his testimony at that time. The reason is, it was recent. While in Reno some of those people there threatened his life at gun point. Someone stepped in and talked the men out of killing Louis and then he got on his bike. He went to try and find his friend's house.

We started seeing each other again, He wanted to marry me again, went to marriage counseling and were going to church. We still called each other husband and wife. We always did, even while apart from each other. The counseling went on for months. I started seeing good changes in Louis.

Then after months, suddenly things changed for the worse. Louis, I felt was using drugs again although I couldn't prove it. Somehow I was the one with the problem. Our relationship was slowing down. I tried to talk to him about his drug program, but he didn't want to hear it. He started acting strange again and what I believed happened, was he started dibble dabbling in drugs just a little. But this "little bit" changed his personality into that selfish, mean spirited man again.

You cannot lie to God. The Holy Spirit within a Christian is an amazing thing. He gives us discernment. We can discern when something is of God or it's from the enemy. Remember I grew up around drugs, used them myself. It was pretty hard to fool me. One thing my husband always tried to do was make me think I was crazy for even asking if he was using. I had already opened my heart and my kids to him. We were ready to trust Louis again. But he was lying and I knew it. This was so difficult. It must have been confusing for the Christians who were praying for us, when we got back together and for our kids.

Chapter 24

Matthew 12:43–45 (NLT)

"When an evil spirit leaves a person, it goes into the desert, seeking rest but finding none. Then it says, 'I will return to the person I came from.' So it returns and finds its former home empty, swept, and in order. Then the spirit finds seven other spirits more evil than itself, and they all enter the person and live there. And so that person is worse off than before. That will be the experience of this evil generation."

Demons are real.

One day, when I was home alone, Louis came by my house and started manifesting demons. Now I believe drug abuse is a gateway for the demonic to come in and out of our lives. Louis was definitely making bad choices. Again, the scripture says

(Matthew 12:43–45, New Living Translation) "When an evil spirit leaves a person, it goes into the desert, seeking rest but finding none." Then it says, 'I will return to the person I came from.' So it returns and finds its former home empty, swept, and clean. Then the spirit finds seven other spirits more evil than itself, and they all enter the person and live there. And so that person is worse off than before. That will be the experience of this evil generation. What Louis had done I believe is get all cleaned up but all too quickly returned to his former ways. The devil overcame him even to a greater magnitude now. He manifested in front of me. He had black holes in his eyes that seemed soulless. He stood up, this large man in a demonic voice and said, "We are legion, What do you want him for? Look at all he's done to you, stop praying for him!" I had thought, now I know I'm doing the right thing, the devil is afraid.

"Close the windows, close the doors you're all alone. "The demons said these things to me.

I yelled," Liar Devil the Lord Jesus is with me!" I rebuked him and Louis laid down like a zombie and shut his eyes but he kept manifesting. Soon other ministers came. The first was my friend Mary. The demons started trying to talk to her and then more prayer warriors came. We all prayed for a longtime until he seemed to get better.

When we were done praying, I told him "I think you need a drug program, it's going to be hard to make it out here without help."

We knew of some Christian programs that could really work with Louis. It was apparent to all of us that the drugs were the vice Satan used to hold him captive. But he didn't want to go and his family wasn't keen on the idea either. He returned to his mother's home. Days passed without much word from Louis. Until one day I got a call from my mother in law saying, "Please come, Louis tried to take his life." She sounded scared. She didn't call the police because she was afraid they would take him to a mental hospital.

So I went to his moms where he was living. His brother was there, he seemed very untrusting towards me. I guess he didn't know or understand that I had a heart of love and the best intentions for his brother Louis.

So I saw Louis lying there on the ground. He was out of it. His face looked discolored and the veins looked like they had popped all over his face. His family had found a suicide note on the car saying," I'm sorry, please forgive me."

He had shut the door to the garage and tried to suck on the tail pipe while the engine was running. Unconscious, his family pulled him out. After they found him they had called me to come. I came with a friend to see how I could help. We made some phone calls and got Louis into a well know Christian drug and alcohol abuse men's home. The program took him right in.

Days later I got a phone call from them saying, "Louis is on the roof of two story building sitting on the ledge "they asked me what they should do. I told them to put me on the phone with him and to go tell Louis I want to talk to him. Right after they called me he finally got down off the roof.

They had to call the authorities and they took him to a mental hospital. His family wasn't happy about this. I told them "Whatever it takes to help him is what should be done." He obviously needed help. He was sent to the mental hospital and put on heavy medications. One thing they diagnosed him with was being psychotic amongst other things. All this was so hard to hear. Everything looked and seemed so hopeless. We had prayed and prayed for many years for Louis and now this!

I went to see him when they had transferred him to another mental facility. He was there for three months. I was shocked at how mindless he seemed. Like a zombie walking around, he didn't even notice I was there. He couldn't even talk to me he was on so many different drugs. There was no more Louis just the shell of a man standing there. I can't even describe how sad this made me, except to say this broke my heart. No one would have blamed me if I had just walked away from him for good because of all I went through with him, but I didn't give up. Jesus didn't give up on me. If all I could do was pray and keep my hands out of it, so be it. God knows what he's doing. I certainly felt helpless but I couldn't get it out of my head, the fact that the devil was worried. "Why do you want him? Look at all he has done to you. Stop praying for him." It seemed to me that I should do the opposite of what the devil wanted.

Louis stayed in the facility for about four months and received help for his depression and disorders. When he came out we saw each other. But soon we were drifting apart. We didn't see much of Louis anymore. I was still praying for him. We were engaged but that was definitely not going to happen, so I put it all on the back burner and got back to just praying and taking care of my family.

I didn't recognize it for many years, but some people who have mental health issues will attempt to self-medicate. There are chemical imbalances in some people for a variety of reasons. So you may need medical help to get through this.

People with addictions have spiritual strong holds in their lives. The power of God can deliver you. But be careful not to return to those habits once God has delivered you. Those spirits don't want to let go of you. In fact, once you've been delivered, if you return to vomiting, you may inherit more demons, stronger then the first ones you were delivered from. They don't want to let you go.

Stand strong in the Lord. Ask for help, don't go through this alone. We all need a support system in our lives, friends and people of faith around us.

You can't go rescue your friends or relatives with an addiction if you're struggling yourself.

The bible says, *"Then Jesus gave the following illustration: "Can one blind person lead another? Won't they both fall into a ditch?" (Luke 6:39 NLT)*

They can't. Pray for these people. You may have to stay away from old friends, hang outs and loss some numbers in order to

put up boundaries in your life. You need to build spiritual muscle. Get healed in your body and your spirit.

If you've had any kind of addiction and your now clean. Start taking doctor recommended supplements and restore your body.

If you lived as an addict for a while just remember it may take some time to start feeling better, even in your mind.

As an ex drug addict myself I have found that quality time with Jesus, reading the Bible and prayer has a calming and peaceful effect on my body.

Ask for prayer if you need it. Find a good Bible believing church and be encouraged.

Chapter 25

1 John 4:4 (NIV)

"You, dear children, are from God and have overcome them, because the one who is in you is greater than the one who is in the world."

Matthew 12:43–47 (MSG)

"When a defiling evil spirit is expelled from someone, it drifts along through the desert looking for an oasis, some unsuspecting soul it can bedevil. When it doesn't find anyone, it says, 'I'll go back to my old haunt.' On return it finds the person spotlessly clean, but vacant. It then runs out and rounds up seven other spirits—eviler than itself—and they all move in, whooping it up. That person ends up far worse off than if he'd never gotten cleaned up in the first place. That's

what this generation is like: You may think you have cleaned out the junk from your lives and gotten ready for God, but you weren't hospitable to my kingdom message, and now all the devils are moving back in."

Proverbs 26:11 (NLT)

"As a dog returns to its vomit, so a fool repeats his foolishness."

One night I went out to get gas with all my kids in the car. I didn't usually go out at night with my kids, but on this night I did. I pulled up and there was Louis with a platinum blonde woman in his truck, both were wearing matching biker outfits, I walked to the driver's side, where Louis was sitting and said to him, "Louis, who is this woman?" The lady started bobbing her head defensively and said, "I'm Shelley!"

I said, "Do you know who I am?"

She said, "Yes, I do! "

I said, "So you know we are engaged to be married again." I turned to Louis and said, "How could you?"

"What about your promise to me and your kids Louis you told them you would make us a family again now here I find you with another woman!"

He then tried to take off fast in his truck.

I didn't know the kids got out of the car and Shelley screamed, "Stop the kids!" Her yell stopped Louis from hurting the kids. As strange as it sounds, I was thankful that she had the decency to scream and stop him from hurting the children. I walked up to the window and at this point I could feel the Holy Spirit so strong helping me.

I looked at Shelley and said, "I will not hold this against you, I forgive you. I'm a Christian woman, Shelley." Then I turned my attention to Louis, looking at him and standing on the driver's side I told him, "Louis, you made promises to your family and you've broken them again." I walked off with our kids and I was crying. I prayed for God to get us to Carol and Matthew's safely — we needed prayer. We went to their home and they were very kind to us.

I dreaded waiting for him to change and knowing he found someone else.

I truly appreciated the prayers of the Christians in my life. What a blessing it had been to me and the kids. I understood why some of them did not care for Louis. He had done a lot of bad things to me and our kids. I must have been frustrating to see me continually suffer.

But I had a word in my heart from the Lord. My job was only to believe. To keep living for The Lord and raise my kids to know him.

Just because I was believing for a miracle and even suffered from a broken heart, it was not an excuse to stop living a good life.

But I was lonely for someone to talk to about this situation. The friends I had just could not deal with it. My having faith in my heart for a miracle really bothered them. So for the most part I had stopped talking with or trusting them with this part of my heart.

I needed to go to the library one day so I packed up my family and we went. I was so discouraged at this point because of my situation with Louis. I knew what God told me when I heard his voice and I felt in my heart that we would be restored one day, but it was getting to be so difficult.

I kept my emotions to myself, which was lonely. I only brought it up to God. As much as I loved Carol and looked up to her I knew she wouldn't understand me. Carol always had a really good marriage and a supporting husband. She made plenty of remarks that sometimes hurt my heart regarding Louis.

So I prayed to God he would send me someone who would be willing to stand with me. I asked the Lord to send me someone who understood my heart for Louis. I prayed while sitting by the window of the library. About an hour later I got up to leave the library with my kids and I saw a woman with a familiar face walking into the library.

I stopped her and said to this woman, "You're that lady!" "You're the answer to my prayer!" She looked a little taken back and later she told me she thought, "Who is this crazy woman?" I then explained to her where I had seen her and why she was the answer to my prayer. I explained, "About three or four years ago I was visiting a church.

I was there with my husband. On the big screen we were watching miracle testimonies and I remember you and your husband's story well. For some reason it stood out to me. Your husband had an affair and left you for another woman and you prayed for years for him. God restored your marriage. My husband and I were still together then, but for some reason I never forgot your face and your story. It really was inspiring."

I explained that I was in the library, feeling so lonely and I needed encouragement. So I prayed while in the library for help from the lord. I asked that he would send me encouragement and you are the answer to my prayer! The lady's name was Suze, a lady about the same age as Carol. She was a mother and grandmother. She looked like a Brunette Barbara Eden to me. I could tell immediately that when I told her about Louis she would link her faith up with mine. And she did just that, I found a friend, a sister in the faith. She had the gift of faith and we talked often from that day forward. The way she prayed for Louis was awesome — we would pray heaping hot coals of conviction on his head.

We would pray a hedge of protection around him, she would pray against the Spirit of enchantment. She told me to call those things that are not as if they were. She also said to negate negative things with positive truth, don't listen to what "they say" not to look at the circumstances. But to look at what God said.

Chapter 26

Proverbs 25:21–23 (NIV)

"If your enemy is hungry, give him food to eat; if he is thirsty, give him water to drink. In doing this, you will heap burning coals on his head, and the Lord will reward you."

I had a comforter on my bed that I liked a lot that I got for a good price. Louis had come over a day or two after I bought it and selfishly said, "Why don't you give me that comforter for my bed?" I thought "Yeah right, so you can sleep with other women." I was quiet. I didn't respond to his request. I let him visit his kids and then he left.

Suze called me and as we prayed I went and laid hands on the blanket. I anointed it with oil while we prayed. I decided in my mind he was worth more than a comforter to me.

Now, I was going to give it to him. Trusting God was with me, the next day I gave him the comforter. The following night Louis called me in a dramatic tone saying, "What did you do to that blanket, I burned all night!"

I said, "What do you mean?" I had been wondering in my mind how God met with Louis this time. He replied, "The blankets burned!" Then Louis calmly and with a peaceful tone said, "And then they bought me great comfort." While talking to him, I was praising the Lord in my heart. The Prophets word over my life about laying hands on things for deliverance was true.

Where I lived I was surrounded by young people, teens and children. One day I was sitting outside and noticed a young Latino boy looking out his window. I said, "Come down honey God has word for you!" This boy named Arturo came down and we talked for hours on my porch. I shared Gods word with him and I just loved him so much. I loved his mom and his sister. When his mom would work at night Arturo's sister Mercedes would stay with me almost every day. We loved Mercedes. She went with me and my family everywhere. We watched over her like she was my own niece. These kids introduced me to more kids and more kids.

I went to family camp as once again a friend from church paid for me and the children's trip. It was a lot for us all so you can imagine I felt so blessed. There was a great purpose in my going. I was clear headed, focused on God. I had such an amazing time with fellow Christians. My children really enjoyed their time at camp.

While in service one evening the minister said, "As you pray you're going to faces of people you've been praying for, God is touching them now and they will end up coming by or calling you." He spoke more and as he did I saw a vision of a young man who was my dear friend's teenaged son. He had tried to hurt himself and was in trouble with the law. God showed me him and I began to weep for him. As I was praying I knew God was moving in his heart too. The boy's name was Roger. When I got home from camp he called me right when I pulled up to my place. He said to me "Lisa I'm ready." He wanted to go to church and Bible study. I called Carol and told her what had happened. He came and then he brought more kids. Baggy pants, tattoos and most of them had not finished school. Oh my goodness if you could have seen these precious boys. So they were the kids society looked down on. They were predominantly Mexican and African American Youth, most of them without dads in the home and with lower income single moms.

Yes, they were like I was growing up, so I had a real Christ like love for these kids. They would come to my apartment day after day. They always brought new kids for me to pray for. Pretty soon some neighbors were saying things to each other about me and these kids. Things like, I had gang members at our apartments and they were afraid and seemed uncomfortable. I heard other silly comments and management didn't look happy to see them day after day. But I felt sorry for the kids. They were so hungry for God and direction for their lives. I just couldn't leave them this way; I had to help them.

I was given a lot of respect among the youth and they came to me for help for many different issues. Some issues were extreme but not dangerous to me and my family. There was a price I paid for all of this. There were certain people who made trouble for me where I lived. But I was determined to obey God and keep loving them all, even the trouble makers.

New kids got saved almost every day. We had such a good time in God. Pretty soon so many youth were coming to Carol and Matthew's for Bible study that they all couldn't fit in their home. We would have at times 50–60 youth in the house sometimes less, sometimes more. Some of these kids had broken homes, parents in prison and other issues. I really could relate to them.

Carol and Matthew put together a home cooked dinner when we would come to their house.

During the week I ministered to youth almost every day of the week. They were physically hungry and spiritually hungry. I was poor with kids of my own and we didn't have much.

I would say, "Lord what will I feed them, I don't have much." God would speak to my heart "use what's in your house." They were not picky at all, so I got very creative with noodles. I always got a "Thank you, Lisa. "

I saw one of the boys almost every day named Warren. Warren was so close to my heart. He was a great dancer. I use to see his face often in prayer. In Warren I saw a great leadership, an ability to gather kids and they would listen to him, he loved me too.

It felt like I had gained a lot of family and that's what they were. I would take them along to other Bible studies and to different events and expose them to more than they were used to. Bible study leaders and I took them to the Raiders football headquarters, a full Gospel Business Men's meeting and to church.

A lot of the kids got baptized at our church. It took a lot of help from other leaders to get them to there. Carol and Matthew were a blessing and helped get them to our church about 45 to 50 minutes away. That day was amazing. To see them all baptized was a big deal.

We would take the youth to church plays. They always liked the plays at our church. Sometimes kids would act up and give us a hard time. But we persevered.

We gained more leaders for Bible study and they all were great and played an important part in all these kid's lives. One important team member was Brother Mark. He was a father, bigger than most of them. He grew up in the same neighborhood many of the kids had grown up in and he knew a lot about what they needed. And so God gave us a team of ministers for our once a week meeting at Carol's home. There they received structure, a meal and a Bible study. We sometimes had several drivers and would go back for more kids so that everyone could come. Sometimes it was hard to get order or to even talk to the kids. At times these kids would say the most amazing things. Roy, a youth tall in stature, was really listening and when he would talk about God it was beautiful. Roy to this day reminds me of a preacher, so dear to my heart. The girls we ministered to were the sweetest kids. I have so many spiritual daughters. They are all beautiful to Jesus. Every one of these kids has a story to tell. Some of their stories would break your heart. I noticed something; if given the chance most every one of these kids loved to help others.

I will never forget two kids after a Bible study saying "Lisa, can we come over, we need prayer." I said, "I just prayed for you." But the kids kept insisting, so I let them come. Those kids left money on my counter. I said, "Where did this money come from?" They responded, "I don't know. Maybe God put it there." I know those kids put it there on my counter to help me out.

I would have help all the time from teenagers. They helped carry in my groceries and take out my garbage. I had a friend who wasn't doing well financially and she needed work done to fix things around her home. A lot of these kids volunteered to help and they worked hard.

One area I helped these youth was to help fill out job applications. I would talk with different business owners and arrange for kids to apply for a job with them.

I have been to court, talked to judges, parents, grandmothers, probation officers, principals, and teachers.

I helped in any way I could, to better their lives. If I needed Carol's help with anything regarding the youth she always tried to help. Carol and I visited many homes where the families had Spiritual problems and we would go and pray.

I had been praying for a meeting with our mayor and police chief. Arturo my teenage neighbor called me and asked if I would go to an award ceremony for him. It was an award for kids who were in trouble and may have done graffiti or something else. In this program they would complete a unique art project with a positive feel to it. The kid's art was displayed in different places in our city, so that others could admire their artwork.

So I asked Arturo who would be there. He said the mayor and chief of police." I'll be there," I told Arturo.

I walked into this meeting with lots of young people, city officials and officers in attendance. There seemed to be an invisible barrier between the youth and the distinguished officials. The youth all stayed on one side of the room, while the officials talked amongst each other. I was talking with Arturo and the other young people about their art.

So I noticed the police chief was making his way toward us. He looked at me and said, "Who are you and how do you know all these kids?" I said, "My name is Lisa Moreno and I love these kids. I take them to Bible study, minister to them at my home, feed them food or whatever they need, I help them."

He looked so amazed at my relationship with young people. I turned to the chief and said, "I'm going to pray for you." The chief said, "Oh, thank you, please pray for me."

I said "No, I'm praying now!" I said Arturo we are going to pray for him. Arturo being a natural leader said, "Come on everyone,

Lisa's going to pray." All the officials were standing there so I said, "Come on, why don't we all pray for our city. Get in a circle and bow your heads." So they all did.

Then we prayed together. The police chief turned to me smiling and laughing and said, "You are so bold, can I come to your Bible study?" I said, "Sure." I got his card.

I arranged with him to come a few weeks after. Carol and Matthew's house was full of ministers from our church. The teens were all there and we started worshipping and praying. In walked the Police chief. Pastor Dan and many leaders and the teens prayed for him. It was awesome. He had a health condition he was struggling with. They all prayed for his health. After it was over and probably a few days later I heard from the chief. He told me he went to the hospital soon after the meeting. He said if wasn't for the prayers of the people he might have died. Carol and I met with him on a personal level over coffee a few times after that. We discussed a family who had been in gangs for years and the mother came to Jesus but was having a hard time with police. I had known this family since I was about 15. Carol and I explained to him that this mother, named Rose, was getting harassed by people who didn't like her family. We were concerned for her. We explained to him that she is now a Christian. He let us know he was going to talk to people and help her out.

He did. The next day Rose let me know for the first time in her life an officer waved at her and said hello.

I was so happy for Rose.

A few prophetic ministers came to Carol's house. They prayed over the people there. A lot of youth came to see these men and women of God; they were so excited. The ministers spoke over the teens and then came to my own kids. I will never forget the words over my own babies. Lani, Louis, Luke and Levi stood there. One prophet said over my boys (Louis) "Prophet" (Levi) "Priest" and (Luke) "King"

The woman minister said over Luke, "He is a good helper doing things other people won't do. Everything he does he does it with Joy. He will do things nobody wants to do and that's how he'll create wealth. He will travel the world helping great names. A lot of his wealth will be through this. He has creative gift it flows through you (pointing at me, his mom). Then I was told "You will have ideas from the Lord that will make great amounts of money. That gift is in him too.

Than the prophets spoke to me. You have big ideas that are going to come into action this year. You have connections with people. Obedience "OH the obedience you are so obedient. Oh yes you are so obedient. A new car an all paid for vehicle. You tell God you need it for ministry. You have sowed many good seeds they are going to come back to you. There is going to be so much you'll have to give some away. Good seeds. Taxes you're going to get back, more than you expected.

They told Louis that he was a prophet and have prophetic dreams and visions.

They told Levi he was a leader and that people would follow him.

Chapter 27

1 Peter 4:4–5 (NLT)

"Of course, your former friends are surprised when you no longer plunge into the flood of wild and destructive things they do. So they slander you. But remember that they will have to face God, who stands ready to judge everyone, both the living and the dead."

Ephesians 6:12 (KJV)

"For we wrestle not against flesh and blood, but against principalities, against powers, against the rulers of the darkness of this world, against spiritual wickedness in high places."

I started homeschooling with Louis's permission when my kids were small. My friend Mary and other Christians I was around during this time in my life really showed me the benefits of homeschooling my children. I had a lot of respect for people who homeschooled their kids. I wanted to copy Mary because her kids were seemed to benefit from it. There was a tremendous dedication that went into homeschooling children. I went to conferences, joined a group of homeschoolers, and listened to homeschool leaders speak. I really tried to be a good Christian mom to my kids.

I wanted to give them everything I didn't have growing up. I taught my kids to read the bible at an early age and we would pray together often.

My personal experience with public schools wasn't great. Louis didn't have a great experience either. I felt pushed through each grade.

I found out that Louis had been living with another woman. This woman was not like any other he had been with before. I mean no disrespect but she was an average woman. Louis had let me know (for some reason) she had her breasts done and was loaded with money. I took it that one of the main reasons he was with this woman was because she could provide for him.

Knowing Louis's lifestyle and taste for drugs I figured she was like his sugar daddy (but a woman).

All of a sudden trouble! I was issued court papers from Louis for custody and demanding my children attend public school. I couldn't believe my homeschooling was being challenged. I paid yearly for protection from homeschool, which was required from the group we were in. The only drawback to this, is that in cases with the other parent disagreeing with homeschooling, they won't represent you.

I was on my own. I couldn't afford an attorney for the custody part of the hearing.

I had a huge file of criminal charges against Louis to prove he was unfit to make any decisions regarding our children. He had very recent drug charges against him. So I brought in all my proof in my big file. Honestly I thought I would win my case because of Louis's behavior.

I prayed and felt confident. At the same time, I was scared because this was the first time I had been to court without at least one person by my side. As afraid as I was to be by myself, I knew God was with me.

So here I was in court and Louis is there with another woman. We started out presenting our cases. The judge overruled the mediator's decision that Louis should not have legal or physical custody anymore. She gave him back the partial legal custody portion in order to rule against me about homeschooling. I was mocked by the judge who seemed angry at me for being a Christian. She said, I was closed minded because of my religion. She told Louis to keep up the good work. She told me, "I am ruling and your kids are going to public school."

The other woman was making comments under her breath, in the back ground when I spoke to the judge. She was seemed to be gloating

Love Never Gives Up

because I was unhappy. I left so upset. As I walked away from court I saw Louis and Debbie leave laughing and happy because they won. They were smacking each other fives and I felt so defeated. I didn't understand why God was allowing this. It seemed my enemies were triumphing over me. My kids were my world and I was concerned. To me homeschooling seemed like the right thing to do for them.

I was talking to God in my car saying, "Lord I don't understand, they are mocking me Lord." I cried all the way home. I had to obey the judge. They next day I began the process of putting them in school. Debbie beat me to it and tried to enroll them without me, but she couldn't. Only I could do the things legally that needed to be done for my children. Louis didn't even know the kids correct birthdates so he couldn't sign them up.

It felt like this lady was really trying to take over my life. I wasn't going to let her get to me. I knew she hated me and I did not like her either. But I did not hate her. I made sure that I prayed as Jesus told me too. So I did everything the law required of me for my children's school.

A Prophetic word

Soon it was time for a prophetic conference. At this conference my name was called and they began to pray over me. I was told a few things. One lady said "I'm looking at your badge with your name on it, you are creative and it really bothers you when people aren't creative. (My name was written by me in cool boxed lettering) She said, "I see God using you in the public schools."

She said" You're going to write books and you'll have children's books. You will bring Bible stories into the public schools and they are going to let you because they like you so much. God is going to send you a husband, a strong shoulder to lean on because of all you go through with ministry. God is going to use you in the arts. You're going to have favor with social workers. You have a governmental anointing on you.

Another prophet said I see you in the arts, study the arts, you'll set up puppet shows for children. God will use your arts and crafts, study the arts. You will be known as a woman of faith in your community. Another prophet said to me," You'll start a soup kitchen." "You'll see children who need shoes and coats and you'll figure out a way to get them. "You see children's faces and you will know exactly what they go through at their homes."

"You are a blessing to this house, more people should be like you." "So happy to be in the house of God."

Than a prophet said to me, "You don't have to worry if you'll make the right decisions, you question that." "The steps of a righteous man are ordered by the lord. You have been faithful and one day when you get to heaven you're going to see a plethora, a multitude of people as far as the eye can see who made it because of your faithfulness. ""And you will hear the lord say, "Well done thy Good and faithful servant, you've done well."

There must have been four prophets taking turns speaking. The amazing thing was, that was my private prayer that morning, "I just want to hear you say, Well done thy good and faithful servant! "You've done well with what has been given to you."

I felt so much better. Now I knew God had given me confirmation that HE allowed all that was happening in my life for a greater purpose.

One day Louis had called me and we had a disagreement, nothing out of the ordinary and pretty typical for us at this time. I had a missed call and a voice message, so when I checked it I was surprised that Louis's girlfriend left me a crazy message telling me off. There was really no point to it except to say terrible things to me. It was a disturbing. She ranted and raved that people don't like me, they think I'm crazy. Everyone in the city knows I was insane. She talked about Louis and my poor kids having a mom like me. There was more but you get the idea.

She was out of line; I didn't even know her. We had never even had a conversation before. So I wrote out the court paperwork to keep her from calling me ever again. She may have been dating Louis, but she had no right to even call me. I was not going to let her get away with this bad behavior.

Soon it came time for court with Debbie and Louis came with her. This was a different courthouse and judge. This time I didn't go alone; my BFF Angela was there, my mom, and my dad. I also saw my friend from school, Scott. When I saw Debbie she looked terribly nervous. She kept holding Louis. I felt so much peace, like never before.

I had to get in line to sign in. Debbie and I were standing by each other so I asked my friend Scott to let me go in front of him. So he let me. When I stood up to speak I could feel my Lord with me. I explained to the judge what had happened and told him I have nothing against her. I said to the judge, "I don't hate her. I don't even know her. I just want her to leave my family alone." I also let the judge know that Louis does not currently get to see his kids because of drug charges. Louis started yelling in the court that I couldn't say that about him. He got in trouble with the judge, who firmly warned him to stop yelling. Debbie really got scolded. The judge said to her "You cannot interfere with them, these are their children they had together and you'll have to deal with it."

He warned her not to harass me again. She said to the judge that Louis was her fiancé and some small talk. The judge let it be known he meant what he said and that he did not want to see her in there again for this.

My friend Angela said to me, "Lisa, he couldn't keep his eyes off you. He had such adoration in his eyes for you. He didn't even look at Debbie—he still loves you." The whole time I stood there I knew he was staring at me. I said to Angela, "I know, I've always known he still loves me."

I didn't hear from Louis for a while after this.

During this time my brother was living on the streets. He was married and had three children with his wife, but he had made some bad decisions in his life. He had come upon hard times and lost it all.

A lot of the youth whom I ministered to, would run into my brother. He had away with young people. He had the same charisma in life I seemed to have. I knew my brother was called to be an evangelist. Even though he was an alcoholic, he was very loving. He believed in God but had a serious addiction.

When I would see him with many other homeless people, I would stop by. He would always say, "Sis, get out of your car and come and pray for these people!" So I would. I would get out and pray. He was always concerned about the homeless people.

Once I went out to check on my brother and he said words I to me I cannot get out of my head. He said, "Sis, you have to help them! You have to start a soup kitchen!" I cannot forget his cry. It was like God used his mouth to help me see, the great need of these homeless people. Already God had me feeding homeless kids, from my home. Young people passed the word along that there was a lady that will help you. So they came, young people, even a few young adults without a home would come for a meal and prayer. I had learned at this point how to live on a little or make things stretch.

I found out years later that my great grandmother from Puerto Rico would feed the poor and the homeless even though her husband had died. She too had lots of children.

Sometimes I would go visit my brother and he would be hungry, but he didn't want to eat in front of his friends. He would either share his meal with them or I would bring enough to share, knowing he always had friends with him. He used to tell me, "Sis, one day I am going to help you in your ministry to kids." I always believed he would, too.

My brother's stomach began to look as if he had a big basketball in it. It was so big from drinking. He always was a strikingly handsome man, but now he was looking unhealthy. I always feared he would get sick from drinking or worse. I started talking to my brother about getting into a program. My parents and I tried to get him in there, but he wasn't ready. I was close to my brother's daughter and I was worried about her growing up without her dad. I expressed this to my brother. I told him that he needed to get clean and then be there for his kids. He wouldn't change. He had no home and his alcohol addiction was getting worse.

My teenagers and some of the moms that I ministered to started having dreams. The Bible talks about these things in the book of Joel. One of the teenage boys said to me, "Lisa I had a dream. In my dream you were driving a Jumbo jet and I was the co-pilot." He said, "We had lots of teens with us. We were flying all around the world. We stopped in Mexico, I saw the signs billboards with the words in Spanish. You picked up more kids there. Then we stopped in China and we picked up more. We even had white kids Lisa! (most kids I ministered to were either African American or Latino)

He went on to say that the sky was dark. That there were people running and screaming, but not us, we were okay. We were all going to heaven.

Another youth had a dream. He had a dream of a decision he must make. He had choice of one thing. He saw God, Me and Carol, a room full of money and the last choice was his friends. He said he chose his friends.

When his friend Robb heard him tell his dream, he said to him, "Man you should of chose God, Lisa and Carol we would of all followed you there anyways.

Around the time everyone else started having dreams, I had one too. I'll never forget it, It was vivid and real.

In my dream I saw a three story building, like the apartments I was living in at the time. I was up in the top floor of the building. I was standing there and I looked back and I saw two of the girls that I would minister to, who are my neighbors. I also saw their mom and with them thousands of people as far as my eyes could see and behind them. I saw huge flames of fire behind the people coming close. The building was on fire and everyone was in danger of burning up. I said with a shout," Come I know the way out!" I was the only one who knew the way and I thought they were all following me. I got to the bottom of the building and outside. I looked up to the top of the building, there they all were still in the burning building. They all were in danger of dying from the fire. I then heard the Lord say to me, "Go back and get them and make sure they get out!" I woke up and I was amazed at my dream. I prayed for more understanding of what it all could mean. God led me to scripture.

Jude 1:22–23 (NLT)

> *"And you must show mercy to[a] those whose faith is 'wavering. Rescue others by snatching them from the flames of judgment. Show mercy to still others, but do so with great caution, hating the sins that contaminate their lives."*

After reading that, I understood even more the call God had on my life. God was concerned about the souls of the people within my sphere of influence. I started praying even more for the people. I could see now that one time praying or teaching wouldn't cut it, people needed someone to walk with them through life. Discipleship was a key.

My heart started to be moved with compassion for the lost even more. I would take kids with me everywhere. I would hold lots of Bible studies at any given time on my porch. I saw numerous young people and their families come to Jesus. People dealt with every kind of problem you could imagine and we got the hard cases. I would always bring the kids to Carol and Matthew's home one day a week. I greatly appreciated their help and the others God sent to help.

Meanwhile my children and I continued to pray for their dad. We had heard that Louis was going to marry this woman he was with. I would see them driving all over the place together. When I would see them together, I would just pray because it hurt my heart. I had heard negative remarks again and again through all the years of praying and believing for him. I never once received took their advice to heart, I knew what God had told me and that was good enough for me. God didn't tell them what he had told me about Louis, so how could they understand. It may have sounded like foolishness to them, to hear again what I was believing for.

I had heard Louis and the other woman were now going to church together. The funny thing is at that time he was still in a biker gang, using drugs and not helping me with the kids financially. So I thought I'm going to keep praying for a heart change in him. I was going to hold on to the word God gave me years ago at my mom's house. I decided that I would go with my friend Angela, to the church Louis was now attending. My friend Angela knew some of the ministers at his church and she use to be a member there. I thought, "Well if they are led by the spirit, they will understand what I'm trying to say to them." "I'm going to let his Pastor know I'm a Christian and believing for my family to be restored."

I couldn't get to the Pastor to meet with me, but an elder would." He had known my friend Angela for years. Angela and I were talking with this elder and he was rude. Even though I came with a heart of truth and love for Louis. I tried to explain everything to him. He did not care. He let me know that at this church they protect their people. He said Louis had other plans, that they were a part of his church. I mentioned to him aren't we all the church, Christian's? Didn't it matter that I and his kids have been praying for years for him? He did not care. He was cold.

I think my friend was more upset than I was. This elder was just like Louis and had a praying wife. They were separated for years just like Louis and I. He returned to his wife years later when God got ahold of him. My friend said of him," how quickly he has forgotten all the grace God has given him and his family."

I thought, "Well, he is not God. God said it so that's it."

Chapter 28

Galatians 6:9 (NLT)

> *"So let's not get tired of doing what is good. At just the right time we will reap a harvest of blessing if we don't give up."*

After over 7 years I said to the Lord, "Lord I'm getting tired. It's been many years that I have waited for him, please encourage me. I went to a church the same night, special conference with the Guest speaker Marilyn Hickey. I was so excited because I use to watch her often on television.

She came and pointed me out, "Lady with the blue shirt."

I stood up and she gave me a scripture

> *2 Corinthians 1:20 KJV "For all the promises of God in him are yes, and in him Amen, unto the glory of god by us."*

She then said, "If God told you yes its yes. You just say Yes back to God. From now on you'll be called the Yes Yes woman."

It was all about Louis and I knew it. God did not want me to give up. I knew I was getting close to a miracle. That word was a miracle to me.

MY heart longed for the word of God to come to pass. I knew exactly what god was saying to me. I had already heard his voice, I just needed to say "Yes" to his promise.

I still believed and my heart was strengthened.

I knew that all the years of the "Jobs friends" speaking the opposite of what God had said to me, was a true test of my faith. The real test is with the believers, always trying to convince you and change your mind. The reasoning with you, as if you don't even know the voice of God. I loved Louis and I loved God. Those friends loved God, but they couldn't understand my love for Louis.

One day I got a phone call it was Louis saying, "Lisa! Lisa, I'm sorry. I'm sorry Lisa, I didn't mean it!

I said, "What are you talking about Louis?"

He said, "What I did to your mom!"

I said, "What did you do to her?"

He said, "She was over here and I wasn't nice. Lisa, I'm sorry!"

I said, "Louis, I'm going to call my mom, OK? He said OK.

When I called my mom, she said she was fine. She told me that because I was struggling to pay for my daughter Lani's 8th grade Graduation stuff, she thought she would ask Esperanza to help. My mom had not talked to her in years and of course no one had been on speaking terms for all those years. My mom went on to tell me that Esperanza wasn't going to let her in front door. They stood at Esperanza's front door for a few minutes talking. But when my mother let Esperanza know she was there to talk about Lani, she finally agreed to talk to my mom inside.

When my mom asked for her to help Lani's graduation, she agreed to help. All of a sudden Louis showed into the living room where my mom and Esperanza were sitting.

He started screaming at my mom, he was in a towel and had just got out of the shower. He was yelling at my mom for no reason. Esperanza had to tell him to stop yelling. My mom didn't talk to him, she did not defend herself, but instead thanked Esperanza and left, bypassing Louis.

Within hours of this episode I got a call from a friend named Leila. She said "Lisa, The cops are surrounding Louis and they have guns pointed at him. Then I get another phone call from a friend, Lisa the cops have Louis on the ground guns are pointed at him, tons of cop cars are all around.

Soon after I got another phone call. This time from a bail bondsman who said, "Louis needs your help." I asked what happened. He told me a woman had him arrested. It was a stalking charge. I said, "Why a stalking charge? What?" I said, "Was it the woman he was engaged to?" He said yes.

Louis had vandalized her house. There was nothing I could do to help, but pray.

Finally, I spoke to Louis. He called me form jail. He said, "Lisa, I'm so sorry. I know I don't deserve you or your help, but I'm in trouble." I said, "What happened?" He told me some things he had done. It was all bad. He urinated on her things and broke all her belongings. He had found out what she was up to on her computer. She had been mocking Louis on the internet in conversations with people. She also called Louis with another man on the phone too and they mocked him about an affair they were having with each other.

He was angry because they had mocked him on the phone and publicly.

So I called his mom, who I knew had hated me, but I thought, "Well, he needs help."

I found out when he had a court date. I decided to go. I knew this lady was a drug user. I also knew that Louis was no stalker. None of his family members were going to court to support Louis. His mom Esperanza and his brother said they could not make it to court.

I called his dad and asked for help for Louis. I knew he had the money and could help his son. He did live in another state but would be coming soon to deal with a lot of this.

I told Louis not to worry, that he will get an attorney soon. His arraignment date had come. He did have a public defender. I walked in to the courthouse without any fear. I was determined to have a conversation with the DA. When I walked in the courthouse there was Debbie and her friend. She looked shocked to see me there with my daughter Lani.

He was so happy to see us there. He had a glimmer of hope in his eyes when he looked at me and Lani. But he didn't look at us very long, soon his head was low and he looked defeated. I was praying for him while in there, so was our daughter. While on the stand, Debbie said some things that were pretty rough to hear.

I knew Louis had been rebellious yes, but he was no stalker. This part of her testimony I knew wasn't the truth. She portrayed him as this stalker. After this hearing I got ahold of the DA, a female she was very willing to hear me.

I let her know that of all people I have the most right to be upset with him. He owes me over $80,000 in child support he has put me through it. I told her there is one thing I can't stand. I can't stand how this woman is up there playing a victim, when she is his sugar daddy using her money to buy Louis. I told her she does drugs and has a daughter. I shared with her that Louis told me the websites where she's been online doing perverted stuff.

I told her that this woman is not an honest person. I said to her he is wrong, but she is just as bad. And now she wants him sent to prison, for the maximum sentence?

I said to her, "I think I would know, of all people, if he were a stalker. He has a drug problem yes, a stalker no."

I suggested to her, "Maybe she needs to give you a drug test."

I told her about how she called me in the past causing trouble. I think the DA believed me and what I had to say about all this. She let me know she would be questioning Debbie some more.

Louis's dad came down, hired an attorney and he told me to take charge of this situation for Louis. I said OK.

In this time God was working on Louis, he started going to Bible study in jail everyday. Reading the bible sending letters that were amazing. He was very repentant this time for real.

I knew in my spirit this was it, he really meant it, and he was willing to change. Louis was clean now that he was in jail. He told me everything he had done and I forgave him.

Lani wrote her daddy a letter while he was in there. Louis told me he broke down when he read it. He said her words were so moving that he read it to many inmates in his Bible study group. He said some of the most hardened criminals cried when they heard her words.

Our daughter was wise beyond her years.

Louis was locked up in jail for about 9 month's total. During Thanksgiving we were invited with my parents for Thanksgiving dinner at his mom's house. I brought all my kids and my parents. We enjoyed this time, but we all missed Louis. Louis told me that when he heard we were with his family for Thanksgiving he cried. It meant a lot to him to see the unity.

Louis always had the same prayer, that his mom and I would be friends.

She and I stuck together during this time to help Louis. Helping Louis unified our relationship. She told me a lot about his behavior at home. She talked about his drug use and how crazy his life had gotten because of this. She was finally saying it herself, no more denial.

I asked my sons if they wanted to do this program to get to know there dad again. They would be able to go into the jail and play basketball with their dad. They said yes. When I took them, they loved it.

The DA couldn't let Louis get out without punishment but I think everything I told her really helped Louis. He wasn't going to prison for years like Debbie wanted.

We wrote each other often; he wrote me more, though. We would talk once in a while on the phone.

We started talking about our family and our future. He wanted us to get married again. That's of course what I wanted. In all the years we were apart he always referred to me as his wife and he was my husband. I loved this man with all my heart.

He was so thankful that we still loved him and waited for almost 8 years for him to come back to us.

He felt unworthy of us. And struggled to forgiving himself. He said he had wasted so many years and talked often about all the pain he had caused the kids and me. He said he was an idiot. I went to see him quit a few times in the jail. I didn't like the long lines, the waiting was a lot, but he looked so happy to see me. I brought our kids one time on a regular vising day, but I didn't like the atmosphere. I decided it was best they didn't go to the regular visiting days anymore. The only time I brought our kids to see Louis was on the day they played basketball at the jail with their dad.

I had a lot of things to do back at home. I was a single mom in many ways. I had a large family. I ministered to youth and I was in a relationship with my ex-husband, while he was in jail. I had a lot going on in my life. I did not want to neglect the teens because of my busyness. I prayed for them daily.

Chapter 29

Mark 9:42 (NIV)

> *"If anyone causes one of these little ones—those who*
> *believe in me—to stumble, it would be better for them*
> *if a large millstone were hung around their neck and*
> *they were thrown into the sea."*

Proverbs 31:8 (NIV)

> *"Speak up for those who cannot speak for themselves,*
> *for the rights of all who are destitute."*

One day while walking out to the parking lot of my apartments, I saw an officer in the parking lot, who I had known for years. He said hi to me and told me he sees my brother a lot on the streets.

I asked why he was at our apartment and he let me know it was for another resident a ways down.

I told him about the teens who lived around our apartments, how they are wonderful young people and they go to Bible study.

He said, "Why do they go to Bible study? What are they doing wrong?"

I couldn't believe the ignorance of what he had just said, and the distain in his voice. It hurt me to hear how he viewed the kids.

If a child takes the time to go to Bible study, I think it shows they are trying to improve themselves.

Right then God gave me a vision, a picture. I saw officers in their uniforms, coming to a performance put on for our city. I knew God wanted people to see them as he sees them. This plan of Gods made my heart happy.

They are all talented, loving kids and they could do great things if given the chance. Some of the teens could get out of hand from time to time, but nothing we couldn't deal with. I said to the Lord, "You want a play of some kind don't you Lord?"

I even saw the outfits the kids would wear. I saw how they were designed. Flames of Fire on the skirts to represent the darkness that comes against a youth. I knew our play would have something to do with interpretive dance and the dance would be about the tormented youth and their struggle. Joan, a talented choreographer, and other Christians from church helped out so much. Team members sold tickets, made costumes, gathered donations for a raffle. The team invited a lot of people to come to this event that would be held in a large theatre. The kids practiced for weeks.

There was a lot of work to do and everyone had their part. One of my main functions was to connect with and gather the youth.

Everything our team prayed for regarding this youth event God did.

We wanted the County Fire Chief to speak. That meeting happened because of a Christian man named Lee whose grandchild went to my son's school. One morning I said to God," I don't know how to connect with him. I've tried to call him, please help me."

That same morning while at my son's school, I saw a lady. She was older and looked distraught and confused. I asked if I could pray for her. She said yes. As I was praying I heard a man's voice praying with us. When I was done praying the lady said to me," this is Lee, a good man, a Christian like us."

I talked to Lee for at least an hour in front of the school. He was such a sweet person. I told him about the youth. I told Lee, "There's only one thing I've prayed for, I'm waiting on God for the answer." He said, "What's that? I said I need to ask the County Fire Chief to speak, but I can't get through to him by phone. He said, "Now that I can help you with. I was the chief before him and I mentor the current chief. I talk to him every day! I said, "Really? Praise God!"

Joan, the choreographer, wanted the kids to talk about how they met me. She said it would be called "How I met Lisa." I told her that didn't think that was a good idea. I didn't want anyone to think this was my idea. I wasn't trying to make this about me.

The youth loved the idea and asked me to let them do this. To be honest with you I was afraid of offending Carol. I made sure it was OK with her. She was there with us. So I turned to her and said, "Is this OK with you?"

She said, "Absolutely." So I told them to go ahead and do what they felt to do.

We all have lost our patience. Every one of us is guilty of messing up from time to time. I myself have made a lot of mistakes. If someone continually hurts us, we try to forgive them in our hearts. But should we allow these people to continue to hurt us or others, and never make them accountable for how they act?

We were dealing with children and teens in ministry. I had already protected my kids against a lot of things in their lives. I needed to do this for them even against people I had respected. I believe the Lord was loosing me of needing people's approval. I was going to learn to stand on my own with God. My children would now see a stronger mom. I wasn't going to be so dependent on Carol anymore.

A few things happened that let me know Carol and I were in a different place with each other. On a few occasions she lost her patience. I saw youth just about every day at my home. I knew that the youth were going to bring up Carol being short tempered and yelling a lot at rehearsals. They addressed this to me at my apartment.

We then had another rehearsal and a kid touched the sound equipment. The owner of the equipment warned us not to let anyone touch it. So, when the equipment was touched, not broken, Carol walked up to my son Luke, maybe because he was standing close to the sound equipment. She got in Luke's face finger pointed in it and all. He was about age 11 at the time and she started yelling at him. He looked so intimidated by her. This was done in front of all the youth. I said out loud, "Don't talk to him like that, he didn't do anything." She looked shocked that I would speak to her this way. "What did you say?" I said, "You heard me, don't talk to him that way."

She then said, "I want to talk to you outside!"

I said, "OK."

She was first to talk and said, "You've always shown your kids favoritism."

I said, "Carol, I love all the kids the same. If anything I'm tougher on my kids." I told her, "You were yelling at my son and you embarrassed him and he didn't even do it."

She was so angry with me, but I wasn't going to let her belittle my son.

Carol's personality is strong. She takes charge easily and she doesn't like being corrected. All these years I obeyed her, trying to be respectful to her. For me to speak up was something she wasn't used to.

After that, we said no more about it. We all then continued with our project. But I knew things would not be the same between us. I realized that as I grew in the Lord, I stopped needing Carol's validation. My identity was firmly rooted in Christ. As I stood with the

Lord more, Carol seemed to become angry and attempted to control me more.

That night I had a visitor from a young man at my apartment. He was in tears, afraid to tell me something. Finally, he told me he touched the equipment and he was sorry. He asked me not to tell Grandma Carol (that's what the kids called her) and I promised I wouldn't tell on him. I knew he was sorry.

These kids were thrilled that the day had come for the play. The youth came to me and told me of their excitement that their families would be watching. Our team invited many people to this event. Teachers came, our mayor was there, civic leaders and even police officers. The children were the stars of the show. It was really about them.

The story was an interpretive dance telling the story of a tormented soul torn by the dark ones with the angelic coming to fight the dark forces Our main dancer told me it was exactly how a youth feels. He was dressed as any teen would be and in the dance he was showing the struggle inside, to the song "set me free" it was a powerful choice.

The part of the show came up, "How they met Lisa." Each teen wrote stories out themselves. They were funny stories. They told of my love for them, how I teach them from my porch about Jesus. I felt like a proud parent to see them shine on that stage. The kids got a standing ovation from the audience.

When the show was over we had a meet and greet. We had proud parents everywhere, taking photos with their kids, and meeting civic leaders. These kids did an amazing job!

Till this day children talk about this event, that meant so much to them. I believe it gave them a good childhood memory to reflect on something to carry with them.

Chapter 30

1 Corinthians 7:9 (NLT)

*"But if they can't control themselves, they should go
ahead and marry. It's better to marry than to burn
with lust."*

We were now taking a break for the holidays from Bible
studies at Carol and Matthew's. Louis got out of jail
soon after our event. He spent about 9 months in there. It had been
over 8 years since we first separated. When we saw each other with
our kids, we all cried together. We spent all our time together. We
all had many tears and felt such happiness that daddy was back. We
had one Christmas party at Carol and Matthews with lots of children.
Louis played Santa. The children we ministered to were so happy.
You could tell our own children were so proud of their daddy. He
made a lot of people happy and he so enjoyed doing that.

It felt right this time and we knew he wasn't going to leave us again. Louis had been diligently looking for work. He was trying to find any way he could to provide for us. It was hard for him to find a job because he now had a felony.

We spent Christmas together as a family. It was such a great time. Louis and I cooked together. He loved cooking so much. Our children were happier than they had been in years. Louis and I were so in love. We were always kissing, hugging, crying, and praying.

We got engaged. We had always called each other husband and wife, even when we were not together any more. He told me he had always loved me. I knew he did.

Since Louis wasn't working, and the kids were at school, we were alone a lot and we were intimate. He cried because I had waited all those years for him. Never once did I date or even flirt with another man. In my heart Louis was always my husband.

He didn't feel worthy of me. I knew it was a struggle for him. Forgiving himself, letting us down all those times, wasting so much time. He was hard on himself.

My kids and I saw this man cry every single day, he was so repentant.

We had considered eloping, just bringing our parents and kids. My mom, dad, and other friends said "just marry Lisa." Louis said that would be fine, that we could have a reception later when we could afford it. He just didn't want me to feel bad because of what we had done. He really cared about how I was feeling.

One day, Louis and I went to go visit my parents and all of a sudden he fell to his knees and started wailing, "Please forgive me! I'm so sorry for everything I did to you! To your daughter and my kids! Thank you, thank you for taking care of them! Please forgive me!"

We were all hugging each other. We all cried. God was really healing us as a family. We waited so long for this moment and it was deep. God was doing a profound work in Louis's heart. We all loved Louis with an unconditional love and we all forgave him.

We wanted to marry in our church and wanted to marry with God's blessing. We wanted our friends and family there. As a family we prayed every day and would read the Bible together. Louis would hug us all in his big strong arms and he would cry. I will never forget his sigh of relief as I would lay my head on his chest. He had tears just about every time he took me or the kids in his arms. He said the most beautiful words to us that I will forever hold dear in my heart. He said "You guys are my heart, and how do you live without your heart?"

We went to church as a family. I had waited for years to see this day. One day while we were at church, Carol walked up to me, with Louis standing beside me and our children, she said abruptly, "You need to go to counseling. That's the rule if you want to get married at church." Then she stormed off, Louis looked puzzled and asked me, "What was that about? Is she upset with you?" I made up an excuse for her behavior, as I always did. There was not a drop of love in the delivery of her message to us and I couldn't understand why.

I never told Louis how Carol was negative about me waiting and praying for him over the years. I never told Louis how other people treated me and the kids badly. It not only would have broken his heart; it would have changed his view of Christians. He was a new believer and more fragile than most in some ways. I didn't want that condemnation put on him. Louis and I felt we should get counseling before she even said a thing to us. Some friends wanted us to wait to get married. There were other Christians who thought we should marry soon. But we knew each other intimately. We repented for this, but I knew it would be too hard to stay abstinent.

We already had a family together, and had been married to each other so we didn't want to wait too long. It would be difficult. We had such an attraction to each other. He had always been my husband in my heart. I lived that way for all those years.

Trying to do the right thing, we asked for marriage counseling through the church. I truly wanted counselors who didn't have a pre-judgment of Louis. We met with Maria and Jose. He was a drug counselor and she was someone I had known for years in Christian circles. We really liked these people. Knowing that Maria knew Carol, I asked her not to speak to her about us. I did this because I didn't want her clouded by Carol's lack of support for our marriage.

When we started counseling I noticed something about Jose. He had a glow all over his face. You could see the radiance of the Lord on him. I know Louis really liked him. Louis wanted to change and become the man of God in our lives. We looked forward to our meetings.

I was hurt still because of the relationships Louis had with other women, but we were talking these things out. I still felt he had an issue with wandering eyes. He admitted he always struggled with this and he was sorry and was trying to change.

I asked the counselors if Carol was in touch with her, because some things started making me feel this way. From the beginning I had asked Carol very respectfully not to be involved with or talk to my counselors so there were no prejudgments against Louis. But she lied to me and said she hadn't. I found out later she did talk to our counselors and told them to be tough on us.

I wanted the Lord to lead the counselors and I didn't want her to interfere with that. Trust was becoming more of an issue with Carol and I wondered why she seemed to be so angry with us. She was too involved.

We didn't see eye to eye anymore. I was unsure of how we could go forward in our relationship as friends, if she was going to continue to be unkind towards my family. I felt the trust in our relationship had been broken.

We wanted to set the wedding date for Valentine's Day; the very day we had separated almost 8 years before. We were making plans; my parents were so happy. My grandma and Auntie were buying our wedding cake and I was trying on wedding dresses. When Louis saw me at the bridal store with a dress on, he started crying he was so happy. I thanked God for every day we spent together. He was so funny he suggested I buy a red wedding dress because he loved me in Red. I could just see the looks I might get in that one.

My mom was the most loving and supportive person to Louis and me. She truly loved Louis like a son, she always did. His name was all over her Bible. She would write his name next to scriptures. She would read like a Bible scholar, find scriptures that pertained to him. One story she loved regarding Louis was the Prodigal son. She was very warm and welcoming to him. We were all happy. I would say my mom above everyone else welcomed him back like Jesus would have.

It started to become a confusing time for me and Louis. People were giving their opinions even when we didn't ask for them.

Isaiah 1:18 (NLT) "Come now, let's settle this," says the LORD. "Though your sins are like scarlet, I will make them as white as snow. Though they are red like crimson, I will make them as white as wool.

My friend Suze had a gentle approach to me and Louis and I greatly respected her and her husband. Their marriage was restored. Louis loved her husband Leo. He had a peace on him and Louis liked this about Leo. He wasn't forceful or demanding. His approach was also gentle.

We really wanted them to give us marriage counseling but I never voiced that to our Pastors, so they didn't know that. Leo felt we should just marry and Suze wanted Louis to heal a little more.

When they would talk with us we felt secure and as if we could trust them. We just were trying to move forward in our life together as a family.

Our counselors, Maria and Jose, said they would not give us their blessing to marry on February 14th. They felt we weren't ready.

My, mom, dad and my kids wanted us to just elope. I wanted to elope but felt I would be judged if I did and harshly reprimanded by certain Christians. Some people treated us with unnecessary roughness. Even though some of their advice may have been good, the delivery was very harsh. There were too many opinions. I think we both felt the weight of the world against us.

I then found out I was pregnant. Of course it is never OK to have sex before marriage, but I was repentant. I went to my parents to tell them I was pregnant. They were so happy. Louis's mother was happy, too.

Louis chose a name for the baby out of a bunch that our daughter Lani and I showed him. Louis liked the name Logan for a boy and Lily for a girl.

Louis's dad owned a few homes in Texas and offered Louis a job and a house for our family. I told Louis I didn't want to go yet because the kids needed to finish school. They didn't want to move yet either, they were doing well in school.

I told him to go ahead of us and we would follow soon after school ended. Things weren't exactly the way we planned it. Everything was moving very fast now. Louis still could not get hired because of his criminal record. Lord, we had so much against us.

The truth is people did shun him. This broke my heart. I was so hurt for Louis; he was trying to do what was right.

Chapter 31

Psalm 55:20–21 (MSG)

"And this, my best friend, betrayed his best friends; his life betrayed his word. All my life I've been charmed by his speech, never dreaming he'd turn on me. His words, which were music to my ears, turned to daggers in my heart."

Soon things would get even worse. I had to talk to Carol. I felt I needed to tell her I was pregnant. Why I still felt I needed Carol's approval, I do not know. I would find out through hard lessons that God's grace is bigger than I had ever dreamed and it was not going to come to me from people but through Jesus.

I also felt like the Lord said, "Don't defend yourself." For some reason I needed to hear what she was going to say. Not because she was right but because out of the mouth comes what is in the heart.

I would soon find out what was really in Carols heart towards me. Nothing could have prepared me for this. I told her I was pregnant.

These were her words to me. "Now what are we going to do? I sang your praises before the pastors, they were ready to give you a job at the church. You are going to stand before the youth and confess everything you have done and then you are going to come back under my teaching. And the reason why you are pregnant is because God wasn't going to let you get away with it."

"And you thought the Youth event was all your doing and you took all the credit for it."

I had tears in my eyes,"

I said, "then you really don't know me."

I said, "Carol I told the Lord I was sorry.

I told her, "Are you saying there is no hope for me?"

She told me, "Well if you repent and come back under my teaching . . ."

Lastly I said to her, "If God forgave me, why can't you?"

She was so angry with me and I left feeling a huge pressure of condemnation. For almost 13 years I had really had looked up to Carol. Leaving her home, I felt devastated.

I felt like I was completely separated from God. I was sorry for my sins.

When I met up with Louis at his moms, Louis saw me cry. He asked me what was wrong. I wouldn't share with him anything Carol said. He just thought I was going through it because we were pregnant and had other things going on. I just couldn't bring myself to say how meanly I was treated.

I almost felt as if I could feel the condemnation he must face and battle with every day because of his past. The heaviness (in spirit) I felt was real.

I didn't want him to know everything because I didn't think he could handle it. He was already under so much pressure as it was. He worried every day because he couldn't find any work. He was discouraged and I was worried about him.

Louis told me that day that he wanted to set his affairs in order. He had his Harley Davidson motorcycle at his brothers. Louis had shared with me and our daughter Lani that when he crashed his bike his brother had it fixed. Louis owed him about $3000 for fixing it. He said he could sell it for $6000 to $6500. When we were divorcing, he put the bike under his brother's name so that I couldn't touch it once we settled in court.

He also decided to put his F150 truck on craigslist. He was going to take a small vehicle to get around and look for work. Louis also confessed that he did mess up on drugs recently and he was sorry. I told Louis," Louis we need to tell your mom the truth and you may need to get some help." He decided to do the right thing and confess to his mom. His mom told him she was very disappointed in him.

He told his mom he was selling his truck and Harley. She seemed upset by that. Louis told his mom he was stopping over at his Brother

Joe's house to let him know what he was doing. He then said, "lets drive to Joe's, I need to tell him what I'm doing."

He told me and Lani, "He may try and fight me."

I said, "Louis he has no right to tell you what to do."

Sure enough his brother was waiting. Louis's mom had told him we were coming. I could see Joe's face from the car and he looked angry. Lani had her hand on her dads back and she was praying for him when he faced Joe. I was waiting in the car and I could hear Joe cussing at Louis. He told Louis," you need this bike, you need it!"

Louis had Lani take a photo of the Harley. As Joe told him he needed the Harley. Louis said "NO! What I need to do is take care of my wife and children!"

Joe was cussing at Louis and I was a little nervous. But Lani and I were proud of him for standing his ground. Louis got back in the car and said to me and the kids, "Joe is so selfish and the greediest man I've ever met!"

Chapter 32

Romans 8:38–39 (NIV)

"For I am convinced that neither death nor life, neither angels nor demons,[a] neither the present nor the future, nor any powers, neither height nor depth, nor anything else in all creation, will be able to separate us from the love of God that is in Christ Jesus our Lord."

It felt like such a war all around our little family. Louis had a talk with me at the gas station. I was lifting up a case of water and he said, "Lisa promise me you'll take care of yourself please don't lift heavy things." I said, "OK, Louis, why are you saying this to me?" Later he told our oldest boy, Louis Jr., "Lou, don't give your mom a hard time and take care of her, son." I looked at him and said, "Why are you saying that to him? I'm his parent I'm supposed to take care of him. Louis are you OK?" I told him, "Louis do you think you need a drug program?" He said yes.

He talked to his mom and said that's what he wanted. We called our counselors and they made arrangements for Louis to go the next day to a Christian drug and alcohol program. I called him and said I loved him. For some reason I was extra tired that morning, as if someone gave me a sleeping pill.

Later on in the late morning hours, my daughter played home videos of us with their Dad. My mom and dad felt to drive Louis to meet counselor, instead of me taking him. They were meeting about 25 minutes away.

The counselor's wife, Maria, called me and said, "Louis wouldn't go to the program with Jose. He insisted Jose take him back home. "Well where is Louis? "I asked her. She said, "Jose left him at the store."

Jose had tried to get Louis to go to the program, but Louis insisted he take him back home. The counselor wasn't going to do that.

Louis's Mom called me and said, "Lisa, Where is Louis?" I said, "I'm not sure. The counselors just let me know Louis was refusing to go to the program and the counselor told him he wasn't going to take him home."

She said, "Gosh darn it" and hung up the phone. I called my parents who went back to find him.

We continued to watch old movies and I felt extremely tired. So much was happening in our lives at that time. I couldn't fight the sleepiness that day. I got a phone call from my mom, "Lisa! Louis is dead!" My response as far as I can remember was, "What Mama, no!" She went on speaking so frantically, "Louis's uncle called me, he fell off the bridge! He's dead, Lisa!"

I think I must have dropped the phone and as my kids hard me screaming they ran down the stairs. I was on my knees screaming, "NO! Oh God, Nooo!"

I told my kids after I got ahold of myself and I will never forget their cry as long as I live. Especially the cry of Levi our youngest child, who was just getting to know his dad. "No mama, not my daddy, I love my daddy mama!" I held him so tight. Even as I write this out for you to read I'm crying. It was so hard to see my children crying. We then prayed together, praying he wasn't dead but just hurt.

I was so weak to my knees and my kids and I were just praying. Then, I got a phone call from my Brother in law Joe. He was screaming at me, "What the hell happened, Lisa?" He started swearing and blaming me. I said, "Don't scream at me, Joe! Where is Louis? I want to go to him." He just yelled some more so I hung up. I felt so faint. I had no real answers.

Why would Louis do this? It must have been an accident.

My best friend Angela called me. Angela told me that while she was in the bath, that same hour, she heard the Lord say to her, "Get up and call Lisa." So she did and when she did, she heard my cry and muffled voice. She said she knew something was terribly wrong. A police officer came to my apartment complex and he did confirm for sure Louis had jumped from the overpass in our city onto the freeway. A witness saw him do this. The witness said that he sat there looking down and then leaned forward and fell to his death.

I felt faint as he told me and I believe I lost my balance into the officer and someone else's arms. It felt like a terrible nightmare. We all wailed as we came to realize it was the truth. The officer waited awhile and I sat down crying. I can't remember all their words my kids said, but their faces I cannot forget. Our Louis was gone. I was pregnant and felt so weak as if the blood was not reaching my brain. My friend Angela was with me and she said I seemed in shock when she came to see me. I was outside packing up my kids in the car going to who knows where. I didn't even know.

My daughter Lani, then 15, told Angela please don't let her drive. She said to me, "Lisa, come on. Don't drive." I said "OK." All of a sudden the street to our apartment complex was filled with so many people, friends, a couple of relatives and all the teens that I minister too showed up.

Someone came and told me, Carol is sick in the hospital or she would have come. I said, "OK."

My children and I were being comforted. The love of the teens, friends, and relatives that showed up lifted us and focused us on Jesus.

Then someone handed me the phone. It was Carol. She said, "I'm so sorry Lisa, I would be there for you but I'm so sick in the hospital or I would be there for you." She said, "I took a hit for you."

I said, "I'll pray for you, but I really have to go.

I cared about her, truly, but God had all the people he knew should be with me. I looked at my beloved teenagers and said to them, "I'm so sorry, I know I disappointed you." The youth turned to me and said, "Lisa we love you. Because of you, we know God!" I cried all the more.

I was repentant and thankful to God for showing me mercy. I got to apologize on God's terms to the teens. I got to apologize for my short comings, and all of the condemnation sent out from hell went away. We all cried and loved each other, every person there was such a blessing. I love how God showed up.

Lani, our oldest daughter asked, "Can we sing Hallelujah?" So we got in a large circle and sang holding hands. It was such a soothing peaceful presence of God. How it ended I'm not sure. My dear friend Angela took time out from college to be there through my time of need. She spent the night on my couch. She said as I was in and out of sleep she heard me say, "I don't understand, but I still trust you Lord!" I was talking to God and I was weeping through the night. My friend sat with me because I was having a hard time sleeping and just wept with me. Sometimes that's what we need a friend there to just hold us while we cry. She cared so much about the state of my heart.

He died on a Saturday and church was the next day. My words to my friend Angela were, "Till death do us part, I understand this." I also said, "I've got to get to my God and his people." I said, I'm going to church, I need it now more than ever."

I went, as sleepless as I was and thank goodness I did. I was so blessed by our church family. They were so good to me and I will never forget their help. They rallied around us and everyone prayed. Pastor Dan spoke kind words to us. He also warned "Do not stand in judgement of this family, God loves this family." I felt supported and that they genuinely loved my family.

Some of the members of my church made sure that for the next 30 days people would take turns bringing us meals.

I got a phone call to come and view Louis's body. I choose friends to go along with me and my children. Of course this was a big deal and I was afraid. So I picked people that I trusted to understand how I felt about Louis. Carol said she would go with me to view Louis's body, but I respectfully declined. That was kind of her to ask. A few days before this Carol, in a phone call, had told me I needed to stop being so controlling. We were discussing all that was happening. I asked her to please not talk to me that way. I had seen her in person the day after and again Carol said, "You need to stop being so controlling." I just could not open up to her, even though she was a leader in the church and I should have been able to pour my heart out and receive some understanding.

What I wanted during this time, were people around me who I felt were supportive to me and my love for Louis. If I needed to cry, yell whatever may happen when I saw Louis's body in that casket, I needed to do this. I wanted people around I knew loved me and would allow me to grieve however I needed to. I wanted people we could trust there when my kids saw their dad. They could mourn for him and feel safe. We went at separate times from Louis's family.

My mom drove over to the funeral home with the kids and me. I also took two of my closet friends. It was so hard to walk up to the casket. I went first. Lani right behind me. I saw him lying in a beautiful Silver casket. Lani and I cried and we held each other. It didn't even look like him to me. He had on tons of make up on his face. But the closer I looked the more I realized it was my Louis. It was his beautiful straight jet black hair. I looked closely and recognized His handsome hands and nail beds, and the little bump on the bridge of his nose. These are things only I may have noticed about him. I felt his hands. They were ice cold. He had on thick makeup. The mortician had warned me about this. She had explained that it took a lot of work to make him look that good. His face on one side had caved in because when he fell he hit the ground hard. All of my children cried when they saw their daddy. I don't know exactly how to describe with words the immense pain I felt watching my children in anguish.

It wasn't just that he died that pained me. It was the events before he died that hurt and how he died that hurt. Again I was feeling weak, barely pregnant and now I was the only parent they had left.

We needed to put the program for the funeral together. His family did everything without me for the funeral, after all his dad did pay for it. I had nothing to give. So his dad put me in charge of this program for the funeral. I was thankful they asked for my help. While we were there in the mortuary, I remembered a picture I had seen of a man entering heaven and the Lord embracing him. We had someone from church make the program for his funeral. It was just beautiful.

Soon after this Louis's family asked us over my brother in laws home for dinner. They wanted to give my kids an opportunity to visit their grandpa. When we went over Louis's dad was in the Living room holding my son Levi peacefully watching TV. He looked so content just holding my son. The rest of us were sitting in another room, at a dining table. It was very tense. The atmosphere felt bad. His brother Joe said something to me abruptly, "So, how did you find this counselor?" I had known that Louis's family was angry and blaming Louis' counselor for his death.

It seemed strange to me because I didn't blame him. It wasn't his fault Louis died. Then I started to explain who he was. So Joe started to raise his voice at me. Lani defended me and then Joe's girlfriend snapped and started interfering. Esperanza asked, "Why did the counselor leave him?!"

All of a sudden my daughter and I were taking the heat for their being upset with the counselor. Lani stood up and cried, "Just be quiet, I can't handle this!" So we both left but as I was leaving I told my father in law, "I'm sorry, I have to go!"

I took my kids and we all left crying, out of my brother in law's home. My father in law came behind me and asked what happened, I explained what happened. I could barely talk I was crying so much. That was such a hard experience for my kids and me.

The next day Louis's family informed me that the singers from our church could not sing at his funeral. They were going to sing some of Louis's favorite hymns. Louis's family would only allow us to give pictures and music to play on a screen during the funeral. Joe had his son's babysitter put this together.

Louis's family then had other plans. People were meeting them at Joe's house for dinner, so Louis's family didn't have time to put it together. That suited me just fine. I saw it as an opportunity to do this how I felt Louis would have wanted.

I met Joe in the evening. I sat in my car with my friend Angela and daughter Lani, waiting for him to follow us to the baby sitter's house. My brother in law had a visitor. A woman came out of her car and Louis's mom, his girlfriend and Joe warmly greeted this person. I noticed who she was. She was Louis's ex-girlfriend; the one he had when we were still married, but separated at the time. For some reason this made me feel disrespected. But I was on a mission to honor Louis with this DVD. I had to overlook this. I had to overlook a lot of things.

So I went to the babysitter's house. We took the five pictures of Louis's family gave, along with our family's many pictures. We brought Christian music that Louis loved. What seemed hurtful was a blessing in disguise. This would be a tool God would use to touch hearts at his funeral, I just felt it. God put my eyes back on him and took my eyes off of the past pain. I really was focused now. Joe's son's babysitter was super sweet and did a good job putting this DVD together.

One song we used was "I Can Only Imagine," by Mercy Me. The other two songs were by Jeremy Camp our favorite male Christian Artist. The songs we chose were two that Louis liked, "I Still Believe" and "There Will Be a Day."

Chapter 33

James 1:27 (NLT)

> *"Pure and genuine religion in the sight of God the
> Father means caring for orphans and widows in their
> distress and refusing to let the world corrupt you."*

Exodus 22:22–24 (NIV)

> *"Do not take advantage of the widow or the father-
> less. If you do and they cry out to me, I will certainly
> hear their cry. My anger will be aroused, and I will kill
> you with the sword; your wives will become widows
> and your children fatherless."*

My friends, church family and family did an amazing job, making arrangements for people to bring food to the funeral reception.

My mother in law reserved the hall of a local church. Pastor Dan officiated. Louis always had immense respect for him. The day finally came for the funeral. It took everything I had to pull myself together. My kids and I let he Pastors know that we wanted to speak, so they put us on the itinerary. I saw my dear old friend Mary. She was someone I really missed. She was so good to me. She attended to my every need and was my voice in relaying messages. She was like my lady in waiting. We prayed throughout the funeral together. She brought me comfort. Louis had a lot of respect for Mary.

I heard that there were almost 800 people at the funeral. There wasn't enough room in the building. There was an overflow, so a lot of people were outside and in the halls and even in the parking lot. My family sat on one side and Louis's family on the other.

The video honoring Louis's life played. It was such an amazing piece of work. The music played along with the pictures across the screen. The Holy Spirit was there. It showed Louis through the years. It was moving and you could hear the weeping throughout the room. Then Louis's brother Joe in an obvious state of despair stood up and yelled, "That's my brother!!

Than my children and I got up and said a few words. The only thing I remember saying was, "Fathers be there for your children and don't give up so easily on your marriages. I talked about Louis asking me one day, what would I say at his funeral and what would I say about him. So I told them the good things about Louis. I then prayed for everyone and I even prayed for his ex-girlfriends there, because there was a row of them. All of them were very respectful to me. Then my father in law got up and spoke. He said kind words and thanked everyone. He said, "I know many of you loved Louis." He then said, "Be patient with your children."

Our Pastor then spoke. He talked about Louis; how he wanted to be a good father and husband. He talked about his life. He was just amazing. A few more people got up and spoke and it all was very comforting. When it was all over we thanked everyone for coming and invited them to the reception hall where an enormous amount of food was waiting. My children and I had lots of loved ones around us.

When it came time to go to the grave site, I felt a little faint, being just a month pregnant. I was cold and tired. I watched my older sons Louis and Luke standing there, next to his coffin. It broke my heart to watch my children say goodbye to their dad right before he was put in the ground. Many Pastors and other friends from church gathered around my family. My church was awesome in every way possible. Even as I write this it brings tears to my eyes to think how kind people can be. All of my friends and relatives stuck by my side. I will never forget how many people comforted my children and me. It was the most beautiful funeral I had ever attended. There were so many kind things people did to help, too many to list. One that stood out to me was that friends took excerpts from Louis's letters to me and the kids and photocopied them and placed them on stands around the funeral. I was glad that people could read for themselves all that was in Louis's heart. I wanted everyone to know how he really felt and how he was trying to change. The poster boards had letters from him, where he talked in detail about his love for God. His letters repeatedly told the children and me, how sorry he was for wasting time and being terrible for all those years. His letters to me said I was right about everything; that I was right when I took the kids from him because of his lifestyle. All the things he said helped me remember that he loved us and he was trying to get his heart right with his God and with us. These served as a comfort for me, my family and others who loved Louis.

Louis's father paid for his headstone. It said, "Beloved Brothers Moreno, loving sons and fathers." There were two names: Louis's on one side, and his brother's on the other, for when he dies.

My brother in law Joe put a lock on Louis's room. I asked my mother in law to please allow my children in the room to go through their dad's things. My kids had asked for anything that would bring a memory of him; his smell, his pictures, his clothes. I asked my mother in law to please allow the kids to do this. She explained that Joe wouldn't let us in because Louis had been cutting himself in there and there was blood on the sheets. I told her to cover the bed and let them in. But they continually ignored me or would say no to my request. My mother in law did let me know that Joe and Joe's older son went through all of Louis's belonging, taking what they wanted. This upset my children and me so much. We weren't allowed in there, I was told, until my brother in law could clean the blood.

Joe had left me a phone message saying, "Why don't you drop the kids off at my house at three to see my dad." I sent a text message to Joe asking him about Louis's things, also commenting back about the kids seeing their grandpa. The kids did not want to see their uncle.

Joe called me screaming, He said he was the sole heir of the Moreno estate. I didn't need to worry about these matters and a bunch of swear words. I got off the phone upset. I could have cared less about anything except what rightfully belong to our kids. These were not things of value, except sentimental value to them. No one seemed to care in Louis's family if my kids were OK. Why couldn't he have thought of his niece and nephews' feelings? Didn't he recognize that they just lost their dad?

It was all so very hard for us all.

My 15 year old daughter had enough. She sent him a text, without my knowledge. She said to her uncle, "Don't you ever talk to my mother that way again. She is pregnant with my dad's baby. I don't want to see you ever again."

We met my father in law and mother in law for dinner and they visited their grandkids. At the end of our dinner, my father in law handed me what Lani had written in her text. Joe printed it out and gave it to his dad. He had left out part of it though.

Later, my mother in law called me, she sounded a little frantic. She asked me if I knew where Louis's F150's pink slip was at. Joe and Louis's dad were wanting these things. I knew where the keys were and the pink slip Joe was looking for. Louis had left his truck at his mom's house and had given me the pink slip and the key. All of a sudden, I had great pressure and cramping in my stomach and I started bleeding. I called my doctor. They told me I may be miscarrying but there was really nothing they could do since it was still so early in my pregnancy. I saw the doctor again when I began spotting and I was just told to take it easy. Easier said than done.

We were all so glad we were having a baby. Losing Louis was hard enough, so this little baby gave us all hope. I knew Joe wouldn't give up on harassing me until he got the pick slip. He already had Louis's motorcycle.

I had to look at this issue as a concerned mom for my unborn child. I said to my parents, "I don't want to go to court with them and I know they will fight me. I can't lose this baby, nothing is worth that."

The anger Joe had displayed and the way his parents protected him wasn't good. Not allowing their son to do right by his brother's children was wrong. Now I was going to put them in God's hands. The Lord knew I was tired and weak. I just wanted peace. I called my father in law and said, "I understand you are looking for the pink slip. I have it. Louis gave it to me." I said, "What do you want to happen?"

He said, "I would like to have it back, please. Bring the pink slip to Esperanza." I said "OK." He thanked me and hung up on me.

All of a sudden an overjoyed call came from Joe. "Hey Lisa, yeah, go ahead and drop off the pink slip at my house and hand it to my girlfriend." I said, "Joe, I told your dad I would give it to your mom and that's what I'm going to do." He said OK.

I felt bad but at the same time I felt relieved not to deal with them again.

Our niece Veronica, who is Joe's daughter, was pretty much the only one that kept in contact with us during this time.

Someone from my church, a nice lady named Ellen, remembered that one of the letters that Louis had written to me and the children. It said, "We will be going to Disneyland soon!" We never had a chance to make it. He died before his promise to the kids could ever happen. Ellen started a letter to ask people for donations to send my family to Disneyland, my parents included. I needed my parents help with the kids! The most amazing thing happened! My Christian church friends had raised enough money for all my kids, me, and my parents to go. We got two hotel rooms. We had such a generous gift with plenty of spending money. Ellen collected many pins and lanyards from Disneyland throughout the years, and she gave them all to my kids. We were treated so kindly by our friends. They were true friends.

We left just a month after Louis died. We so needed a break from troubles. We had the best time ever. Our rooms were big with kitchens. My parents loved their room too. We were comfortable and happy. I enjoyed every song I heard while walking through the park. I enjoyed every sight, the shops, the food, and I enjoyed being care-free. I will never forget that trip.

Chapter 34

2 Corinthians 5:8 (NIV)

"We are confident, I say, and would prefer to be away from the body and at home with the Lord."

A few weeks after our trip, I received a phone call to come to the hospital because my little brother Patrick was going to die at any moment. I dropped what I was doing, went to all my kids' schools and picked them up to go with me. The hospital was about 55 minutes away. I went as fast as I could to see my brother. When I got there I saw many family members, all so upset. Patrick was in a coma. He literally had no liver function; it was gone. He was not a candidate for a liver transplant. For three weeks I went back and forth to see my brother. One day he woke up but for a short time. He was startled, but I sat and talked to him. He stared at me and I held his hand. I told Patrick, "I'm going to pray and soon you will see Jesus." I told him," say this in your heart and God will hear you."

As I prayed, Patrick had tears streaming from his eyes. He couldn't talk, but I knew he understood everything I was saying. I held him and told him how much I loved him.

Soon after, he died. He was 35 years old. His funeral was filled with people who loved him. This happened about two months after Louis's death. Louis loved Patrick like a little brother and I knew he was with him in heaven. My church once again came to support us. Pastor Dan did the funeral service. In my family everyone's emotions were raw. People were handling this death differently. I think, for me, it was as if I was just going through the motions. I had peace from God once again just as when Louis died. God showed up in my life to show Himself strong and so comforting just when I needed Him most. I always think about the fact that when there is a death sometimes that's when people are more open to hearing about God. Through both funerals I made myself more available to talk with others about the Lord. It's not that I didn't have pain myself, because I did. But I found that sharing my faith actually built my faith more. I experienced what the Bible says; "His power works best in our weakness." I grew closer in my walk with Him through my pain. I love it that not even our pain is wasted. God turns it all to work for our good.

The day after my brother's funeral my mom's sister died from cancer. My poor mother just lost her son and now this. There were so many funerals in just three months' time.

I received a letter from my church saying they wanted to ordain me, to make me a Reverend. They recognized the ministry I do in my community. I felt so happy inside. In passing, talking with Carol, she said to me regarding being ordained, "I'm surprised they would do this so soon." I think that was a dig but it didn't matter God was doing a new thing in my life.

Carol had a meeting at her house with a lot of people we use to meet with. I didn't invite all the people I used to. My friends wanted me there, at our old meeting ground. I must have been acting different in Carol's eyes. She approached me in her front living room and said, "What is this between us?" I said, "What do you mean?" Things weren't the same between us, but we were polite when we would run into each other. We just weren't close anymore.

A lot of people were in her family room and kitchen and a few were near where we were sitting. She was insisting on talking about the things that had happened between us. She was getting upset because I told her this wasn't the place or the time. I told her there that we should do this in private. She said, "No we are going to talk about this now!" So I didn't have much choice. I said, "OK."

So, I told her that she made me feel horrible when I found out I was pregnant. I told her she acted like a Pharisee. I reminded her of what she said to me the night before Louis died. I said God had forgiven me but she had refused to. She defended herself. She was upset by my words and so I left. There was one friend of mine who heard this conversation. She said, "Lisa, I'm sorry. Why didn't you tell us this was happening?" People had an image that things were perfect in my relationship with Carol. It's not how I wanted to talk about this, but I didn't feel I had a choice.

A few months later we lost Louis Senior's Uncle Larry. Uncle Larry meant a lot to my family. He was the best hairdresser. He had a lot of things he regretted in his life. We had prayed together many times and talked about Jesus before he died. He believed in the Lord and was very receptive to him. He was in his early 50's.

Again another death, my mom's other sister. She came to Christ years earlier when she came out to California for a visit. We had the best talks about God. Then my first cousin who I grew up with passed away soon after; a devastation to our family. He was in his 40's.

I was pregnant through all of this. We were at so many funerals. One day I was at home swollen and tired expecting my little baby to arrive at any time. We decided to call him Logan because that was the name his daddy liked best. I was home and my phone rang. It was an urgent call from my daughter's high school. The woman told me she thought Lani needed to go to the hospital. I rushed out my door, went to the high school and got my baby. She was in so much pain, doubled over saying, "Mom it hurts so bad. So I took her to the ER. I told the doctor, "Lani has Polycystic ovarian syndrome, I wonder if she has a big cyst popping. I think she needs an ultrasound." They listened to me and they performed one. When they looked at the x-rays they found a 10 centimeter cyst on her right ovary. The doctor said she had never seen one so big. She let us know Lani would need surgery to remove this. Right then I prayed to the Lord that he would put me into labor so I could help my daughter. That night I went into labor. The same doctor who would be doing my labor and delivery was the same one who would do Lani's surgery in less than one week's time.

Logan was born, and was he ever a cutie pie. You would think I would have been sad without Louis there with me, but God really had me at ease. Once again I had that peace from God. I enjoyed every moment with my new baby. He was a joy from the moment I saw him. His new life helped my mom, my dad, my children, and me. Many of us somehow felt comforted by Logan. Louis went up and Logan came down.

So, the same doctor that delivered Logan did Lani's surgery to remove this cyst. The surgery was successful. Tissue was sent out to pathology to have it tested for anything abnormal. The doctor felt Lani would be OK. She would need a few weeks to heal. They had to open her stomach up to take this out, it was so big. She had staples across her stomach.

Chapter 35

Revelation 12:11 (NKJV)

"And they overcame him by the blood of the Lamb and by the word of their testimony, and they did not love their lives to the death."

I was taking care of my newborn and Lani. Within a short amount of time I got a phone call from our doctor. This doctor had been my OBGYN and helped Lani in the past with her PCOS. He called and told me He would like to see me in his office. It was urgent and could not wait. I said, "Just tell me what it is, I'll be OK." He told me he felt so bad telling me of all people, because of all we had already been through.

He let me know that Lani had a rare form of Ovarian Cancer and that it was aggressive. He called it Immature Teratoma Grade 3. He called and made arrangements for us to go to a well- known cancer center in a large nearby city. I went down to his office with all of my kids and my parents. He let me know Lani would need another surgery soon and probably some chemo. My feelings were "Just tell me what to do so that I can help my daughter."

Soon after this I had to take Lani to this large city, at least an hour away, in horrific traffic. I left my newborn and other children with my mother and father. In our meeting the doctor informed me how serious Lani's condition was. He was going to remove the fallopian tube and ovary where the cancer was. He let us know we would need to make arrangements with the Children's hospital that specialized in child-hood cancers.

With these kinds of diseases there are a lot of tests that have to be done before surgery. Lani had a list of them to do: MRI'S, blood work, ultrasounds, and more. Lani was a difficult one to draw blood from; it was hard to find her veins. She had gone through so much already. I could tell my little girl was sick. Lani had her surgery and it was suc-cessful. It was close to Christmas time when we went home.

All these events happened in the same year of Louis's death. 2011 was the hardest year of our lives and we weren't done yet.

We soon had an appointment with oncologists at the children's hos-pital. Lani had so many tests done again. She was bruised from being poked so much. She was 15 when she diagnosed. When I found out Lani would not live without chemo, it shook me. I was told that once chemo was over her chances for living were in the 80 percent range. I was informed that Lani would need about five rounds of chemo. While being treated she would stay one week in the hospital. She would get very sick and I would be her nurse while she was home.

I needed encouragement after hearing about this. I left there crying and said said to the Lord, "I need to go see Pastor Dan." I went straight to his office and I cried," please pray for me that I can have strength. I feel like I can't do this."

He and the staff at the church office surrounded Lani, and me in prayer. I felt like he imparted faith into my heart. I now knew I could do this. Having a church family lifting us up in prayer continually made me so happy. The hospital Lani would be staying at was about 10 minutes from our church.

I said to the devil that day, "Satan you are going to be so sorry for what you did to my daughter. I'm going to give you a black eye for what you did to my family! I'm going to pray for so many people in that hospital."

Lani had all her blood checked again before we checked in. She had a broviac implanted in her chest. This is how they would administer medicine, take blood, and give Lani her chemo.

Lani got very close to many of the staff members who were so attentive to her. It wasn't easy to watch her be brought down like she was from all the chemo. Her color seemed a little grey. She slept while they would give her chemo. My little girl went from a lively person to a lifeless person. Lani said she felt like she was dying.

We would go in the hospital for a week and come home for three weeks. She would come home and be lifeless, tired and unable to care for herself. I was trained for weeks like a nurse to take Lani's blood, clean her broviac, and administer medicine through the broviac. Before all this, the sight of blood would send a chill up my spine. I had to get over me. My daughter needed me. I was so afraid to try all this on my own. It was hard to see that tube coming out of my daughter's chest. We had Lani's hair cut from almost to her waist to her shoulders so the shock of her soon to be hair loss wouldn't be as hard to bear. One morning, about three weeks into chemo, Lani had chunks of her beautiful hair all over her bed. We both cried and I held her so tight. Lani has a pretty face and she still was beautiful. I felt bad for her. She was wearing hats all the time and she needed a wig. I had very little money but managed to get enough to buy her such a wig. She looked very pretty in her wig.

One thing about Lani is she adapts well. Lani is very stylish; good with make-up and clothing. She created her own high fashion turban. What a turban! She looked elegant and she learned to draw in her own eye brows because she lost most of them.

At one point, all of my children were very sick, including my baby newborn. Lani had to go into the hospital for treatment. My dear friend Angela took my place and went with her. She really loved my kids and I knew she would take good care of Lani. My little baby really needed care. He had a high fever, along with my other kids. Then I got a fever of 104 and I too was so sick with the flu. My friend Angela called me and said Lani was in bad shape. They had to stop chemo because she had a 106–107 temp. She wasn't feeling good at all. Her immunities were low it was hard for her to fight the flu.

Chapter 36

Ruth 1:3–18 (NIV)

> *Now Elimelek, Naomi's husband, died, and she was left with her two sons. They married Moabite women, one named Orpah and the other Ruth. After they had lived there about ten years, both Mahlon and Kilion also died, and Naomi was left without her two sons and her husband.*
>
> *When Naomi heard in Moab that the Lord had come to the aid of his people by providing food for them, she and her daughters-in-law prepared to return home from there. With her two daughters-in-law she left the place where she had been living and set out on the road that would take them back to the land of Judah. Then Naomi said to her two daughters-in-law, "Go back, each of you, to your mother's home. May the Lord show you kindness, as you have shown kindness to your dead husbands and to me. May the Lord*

grant that each of you will find rest in the home of another husband."

Then she kissed them goodbye and they wept aloud and said to her, "We will go back with you to your people."

But Naomi said, "Return home, my daughters. Why would you come with me? Am I going to have any more sons, who could become your husbands? Return home, my daughters; I am too old to have another husband. Even if I thought there was still hope for me — even if I had a husband tonight and then gave birth to sons — would you wait until they grew up? Would you remain unmarried for them? No, my daughters. It is more bitter for me than for you, because the Lord's hand has turned against me!"

At this they wept aloud again. Then Orpah kissed her mother-in-law goodbye, but Ruth clung to her.

"Look," said Naomi, "your sister-in-law is going back to her people and her gods. Go back with her."

But Ruth replied, "Don't urge me to leave you or to turn back from you. Where you go I will go, and where you stay I will stay. Your people will be my people and your God my God. Where you die I will die, and there I will be buried. May the Lord deal with me, be it ever so severely, if even death separates you and me." When Naomi realized that Ruth was determined to go with her, she stopped urging her.

*S*omething changed in the kids' grandma, Esperanza. She became concerned for Lani during her treatment and surgeries. She was much nicer to me. She would call and check on Lani. She loved my baby Logan. I no longer felt a division between us.

We had been instructed to keep Lani out of the public and away from sick people while she under-went chemo. We did just that but still she got sick. Even I never had the flu so bad myself.

I just prayed to God, "Help me so I can be there for my baby." She needed me and I knew she would be afraid without me by her side. I tried so hard to get better. Even if I wanted to go be by her side sick, the staff will not let me. It would be too risky for the other kids in the hospital. It would not have been fair to them and I wasn't willing to do that. I had to trust God.

My friend Angela had informed me she couldn't stay with Lani any longer. So finally, after the third day I went to be with Lani. When I walked in the room there was my daughter in tears listening to Christmas music, like we do year round. I walked in and she broke down, "Mom!" I held her and told her everything would be OK, mommy is here. Lani was feeling better already and so were my other kids.

There were two ways for me to look at this situation. I was either going to go into a mindset of defeat or I was going to trust

God. It was time to put on all the armor of God and fight! (See Ephesians 6:10) This kind of fighting is done through prayer, standing on God's word and focusing on him. I wasn't going to allow that spirit of fear take any root in my heart. (see 2 Timothy 1:7)

The world tells you to fight with anger, bitterness and un-for-giveness. After all, life has not been fair to you. The devil wants you to have self-pity. I call them the "woe is me." The enemy wants you down low, and his hope is that you'll stay down. You may even here him whisper to you, "You poor, poor thing, that's so sad. No one understands you, you're all alone. No one cares about you."

Satan is a liar, he's the father of lies. He says all these things to keep you from getting the victory. He wants to zap your faith if he can. Don't let him! Rebuke that Devil and start talking differently. Calling those things that are not, as though they were. (See Romans 4:17)

Chapter 37

2 Corinthians 1:6–7 (MSG)

"When we suffer for Jesus, it works out for your healing and salvation. If we are treated well, given a helping hand and encouraging word, that also works to your benefit, spurring you on, face forward, unflinching. Your hard times are also our hard times. When we see that you're just as willing to endure the hard times as to enjoy the good times, we know you're going to make it, no doubt about it."

2 Timothy 4:5 (NLT)

"But you should keep a clear mind in every situation. Don't be afraid of suffering for the Lord. Work at telling others the Good News, and fully carry out the ministry God has given you."

*e*very day it seemed like God gave us divine appointments. I went around the hospital while Lani would sleep; which was a long time. I would find people daily who needed encouragement. Babies and children had leukemia and different kinds of childhood cancers and sickle cell anemia. I would see moms, dads and grandparents crying. The first divine appointment was on the elevator. I walked on after waking up to go down to the cafeteria for coffee and there I found a whole family crying because their baby was very sick. We went up and down in that elevator while I prayed until they felt better. They left with a smile on their faces. God was there with us.

Once there was a lady who had a daughter that was very sick with cancer. This single mom of two was very upset by the lack of empathy from others toward her and her family. She told me she goes to church and works. Her church had not helped her, her family had not helped her and she had no vehicle. She said she was having a hard time making ends meet. She was just downright sick and tired of injustice in her life. I thought, "Lord you'll have to help me help her and pray for her because she is angry!" I felt like the Lord told me, "Pray Lisa." So I did, I asked the Lord for a car for her, that the Lord would send her support and financial help. I asked God to help her feel encouraged for all she was going through with her daughter's illness. I told God afterward that it felt like a dead prayer, that I felt faithless but I prayed anyway. I left that day to see my family and came back a couple of days later to the hospital.

I was in the cafeteria with some friends from church who had come to support us. All of the sudden someone came behind me and lifted me off the ground. I turned around after being put down, and saw it was that lady I had prayed with. She was so thrilled about something. She had a big smile and greeted me so warmly. I said to her, "My friend what happened?" She told me with a huge smile, "Lisa after we prayed I started getting miracles. She said, "after we prayed I went to church. A woman came in who had maybe visited our church once before. This woman said to the Pastor of my church, "I was at home and I heard the Lord tell me go to church and give them your car someone there needs it."

The Pastor said, "I know who this is for." She then told me, "He called me to the front of the church and told the congregation about what I was going through with my daughter's cancer." "He let them know I had to work with no transportation." The Pastor said, "This car is for you! "He then said, "Let's take up an offering for her to help her through this time." She told me that after all this the whole church prayed for her.

She said to me, "you see that table over there? I looked and a table full of people were waving at me.

I said "yes." She told me, "that's my pastor, my father and family." She said, "I'm so happy Lisa, thank you for praying with me. I said, "Praise the Lord!" I teared up because I was so happy for my friend. What a miracle! God was using us in the hospital. It was our missionary field.

While we were there he was working it out so that many could be blessed. My daughter, while getting treated at the hospital, would pray for countless children. Somehow Lani pulled out the strength to pray for very sick little children. She was concerned for them. When Lani would pray there was anointing. She has healing in her hands. I remember a mom came up to me after we prayed. Her daughter's numbers weren't good so we prayed. While we were visiting friends in the parent's waiting room, this woman came in crying. Her daughter was better! She was getting stronger! They had been there for two years and now were able to go home. I thanked the Lord. It seemed like every day when we were there God had someone for us to pray for. And that felt good!

One evening my daughter and I were worshipping in her room. We did this often and many parents joined us at times. On this night it was Lani and I worshipping when a security guard walked in and he said, "You're Christians!" I said, "Yes we are!" He said, "I haven't seen Christians since I moved to California." Right then I discerned this man was very depressed and that he wasn't happy living anymore.

I said, "Let us pray for you." My daughter and I started praying and this tall man was in tears, God was touching him right there in Lani's hospital room.

We had a friend that would come to the hospital a few times a week, always bringing us a healthy drink of fresh pressed juice. We always enjoyed her company. Another group of friends would come visit after church. We would have church in that hospital. This family had the gift of song. They would worship and the other patients, their parents and the staff loved it. They always prayed with us before they left.

I saw none of my family members during this time come and visit Lani. No one, except my parents, Louis's mom and our niece on Louis's side, came. The primary people that cared for us during this time were our Christian brothers and sisters. People from not just our church but many churches came and they were very concerned for Lani's health.

Being in that hospital wasn't easy, especially for such an extended time. We were always excited whenever anyone came to visit.

Chapter 38

2 Timothy 4:5 (NLT)

> *"But you should keep a clear mind in every situation. Don't be afraid of suffering for the Lord. Work at telling others the Good News, and fully carry out the ministry God has given you."*

*L*ani had just started school again. She was having more health issues and needed another surgery. This time because her oncologist found two more large cysts on her remaining ovary.

We made arrangements for surgery at the hospital in the nearby large city. When we went, we decided to stay the night in a hotel the night before, since 3 a.m. was too early to drive for me. The night before surgery we met with our good friends, who had been there for us during Lani's chemo.

We all went to dinner. They have a daughter Lani's age. Lani, the mom Ruth and I went. We were in the square with lots of shops. After dinner we decided to go to a large makeup shop. It was packed. The music was playing in the store and we started to look around. I was standing there and a young man who worked there, a makeup artist in his early 20's, was staring at me. He had tears in his eyes and walked up to me while I was standing in the store with my friend. He said, with tears in his eyes, "Why do I feel like I know you?"

I looked at him and said, "Honey, that's the Lord. Who is a Christian in your family? Our meeting is an answer to their prayers." He explained that his grandmother, who had died, meant a lot to him, and she was a Christian. I got to lead this young man to the Lord. My friend Ruth and I prayed for him together. We talked for a little bit. God was really touching him in that place. Then he went and got another makeup artist and said, "Can you pray for her too?" So Ruth and I prayed for her as well. She got touched by God right in the store. Ruth had some words of knowledge. The girl had happy tears.

We went to the hospital for Lani's surgery. We weren't worried, even though the doctors were testing her for cancer. We were about Gods business and we all had great peace. Lani did not have cancer. She was fine, thank God. He had her in his hands.

We have an annual Christmas party for the underprivileged in the city where I live. My kids help me with this for months. They are very patient with their mom as I minister to people during the year too. I started praying for a break for my family. We really needed a fun get away. Once again, a friend from church helped raise some money to send us to Disneyland. I still needed more cash or we couldn't go.

We wanted to go for Thanksgiving. It would be decorated for Christmas time during Thanksgiving. We found a great deal, across the street from the park that even served free breakfast. That's no small thing when you have five kids! Three of our birthdays are this time of year, including mine. So we found all kinds of coupons for free dinners, sandwiches, and desserts. All of these places were around Disneyland. My daughter Lani is so organized! We made sure our room had a refrigerator so we could make our own lunches.

One thing God has always placed in my heart is a love for the lost. This is probably the most important mission for us on this earth. Yes, for us to be saved, but also that we continue the work by sharing our faith in Christ whenever an opportunity arises. God is moved by faith. Take a chance and share, don't fear rejection. You will be surprised how encouraged people will be by you taking the time to care about them. He loves the sinners and wants everyone to be saved.

2 Timothy 4:5 NLT But you should keep a clear mind in every situation. Don't be afraid of suffering for the Lord. Work at telling others the Good News, and fully carry out the ministry God has given you.

I knew we needed money so I hustled. I have been painting windows for Christmas since I was about seventeen. I used my artistic ability to make some money. I told my kids, let's go! We packed up the truck and went to work. I went to a small city about 45 minutes away to see if I could get some painting jobs. I was passing a biker bar; one that I loathed. Louis use to go there to party with his biker club friends. Women were always around him. I didn't want anything to do with this place, but I felt a nudge from the Lord. It was a go from God. My older kids were with me. I said, "Stay in the truck, I'll be right back." I felt bold!

I saw a bar full of people. I walked up to the bartender, told her what I was there for. I wanted to see if the owner wanted his windows painted. She said go to the back. There was a small office in the back of the bar.

I saw the owner sitting in his small office. He was a big, muscular Caucasian man in his early 50's. He had lots of tattoos on his body. I told him that I was painting windows and I asked if he wanted his done. As I looked at him I discerned he was in the hour of decision. I now knew I was there for a divine purpose. He said, "You know, after 20 years of owning this place I'm thinking of selling it."

I started talking about Jesus and all he has done for me and my family. I told him about Louis and this bar. I told him that I ministered to youth and all the good things God was doing in my life.

He was so touched. He grabbed some money that was pinned on his board. He said, "Here, You work for God. You don't have to paint my windows."

I said, "Now I'm going to do something for you. Let's pray. Close your eyes." I led this man to the Lord and he believed.

When we got done praying the man said, "I feel so much better!" I said, "That's Jesus." We talked a few more minutes about going to church. I did give him this piece of advice. I say it often: please don't expect the people in church to be perfect. They won't be, but most of them are there because they love the Lord. Always remember to let Jesus be your example.

When I started walking out I had to go through the bar. Then a man sat the bar said to me, "Hey, what's your name?" I boldly said, "My name is Lisa and I'm a reverend!" A man at the bar started laughing at my comeback and he said, "Well, we all need prayer!" I said, "Well, come on everybody, let's pray!"

The bartender came around and said she needed prayer. Every person in that bar gathered in a circle to pray. Only one lady sitting at the bar said, "I don't pray." I said, "That's okay!" I continued with what I was doing. I talked about Jesus to them and then I prayed. The woman who said she wouldn't pray said, "Amen. I prayed too." I said, "Amen!" Everyone was rejoicing. We hugged, blessed each other, and said, "Happy Thanksgiving" to each other.

I got in my truck and my kids were laughing, "Mom we could hear you praying for the whole bar from the street!"

We went to Disneyland two days later and had the time of our lives!

Matthew 18:19 (NIV)

"Again, truly I tell you that if two of you on earth agree about anything they ask for, it will be done for them by my Father in heaven."

Our Pastor Derrin knew my daughter was going through a new trial. He prayed for Lani and he suggested we go to a church up north, that's known for it's healing ministry. Lani was losing her sight in one eye due to the side effects of chemo. We went to a service there and Lani was prayed for. The Lord healed her right there, one hundred percent. She doesn't even need glasses anymore. My son Louis also got prayer for his back. He was always in pain because of scoliosis. The huge lump was gone, the back pain too.

My dad and mom have been the best grandparents. Since Louis has passed away we see my dad all the time. My little Logan adores him. It's amazing how he couldn't really be there for me through my adolescence but he has been there for my kids. This is another place in my life that God has taken the things the enemy meant for evil, and turned it for good.

Also my kid's grandmother Esperanza has changed. She is a good grandmother. My kids love her and she and I have a better relationship.

I have forgiven those who have hurt us in the past, our life has gone on. We have the Lord and he has done a real work in our hearts. I have finally written the book that Louis said I would one day write.

I know I will see him again in heaven.

In retrospect, writing these stories has helped bring healing into my life. Helping other people helps me, so it made sense to write a book. I hope in some way, my story has helped bring healing and hope to you.

Remember Jesus is the Love that never gives up!

Lisa Moreno can be contacted for speaking and book signing engagements at the email below:

LoveNeverGivesUp5@aol.com

Please visit Lisa's blog:

www.5KidsEmptyFridge.com

be obtained